THE **SHRIEK** I DO **REMEMBER**

WINNING THE RACE
OF LIFE AND
OTHER STORIES

BRIAN SLUGA

Two Penny Publishing
1209 SE 21st Avenue
Cape Coral, FL 33990
TwoPennyPublishing.com
info@TwoPennyPublishing.com

Paperback: 978-1-965341-16-2

eBook also available

FIRST EDITION

Two Penny Publishing is a partnership publisher of a variety of genres. We help first-time and seasoned authors share their stories, passion, knowledge, and experiences that help others grow and learn. Please visit our website: TwoPennyPublishing.com if you would like us to consider your manuscript or book idea for publishing.

"This is the true story of one man's struggle for life over death. Brian recounts his state of mind from receiving the crushing diagnosis, a seeming death sentence for an active young man, through his therapy and the long recovery to physical and mental well-being. Hopefully, his recounting of this trying period in his life will serve as inspiration for other people facing challenges in their own lives."

Judson Snow, MD

"I have had an exceptionally good relationship with Brian over the years since his diagnosis. Prior to 1980, testicular cancer was an atypical disease with an extremely poor prognosis. As I watched Brian navigate through the diagnosis and treatment, it was truly clear that he was a survivor. Watching him flourish throughout his life has given me a great deal of joy. My hope is that when people read this book, they realize that cancer is not always a death sentence, just another obstacle we must overcome while living our lives to the fullest."

Joseph J. Banno, MD
Midwest Urological, Peoria, Illinois

I dedicate this book to my loving wife, Maureen,
and to my parents, Tom and Dolores.

A special note to my mother, who, when I told her I loved
her, would always say, "I love you more." Mom, looking down
from Heaven, I hope this book makes you proud.

CONTENTS

PREFACE

This is my memoir, my underpinned idea of family, friends, and feelings.

Testicular cancer is no joking matter. By extension, cancer influenced my life and still does today, many years later. I have learned to adjust as circumstances changed, persevere when it was easier to give up, and come back from the brink of uneasiness as my life was spinning out of control. I wrote this book from my own firsthand experience to help all men and families with their own struggles.

As Hemingway said about love, "It's always the same but always different." That is how I feel when people ask about my testicular cancer. My experience is much the same as others with this form of cancer, yet different from everyone else. The difference is in how I now live life.

Laugh and cry with me, and get a feel of the thoughts that follow me through my days and years. You should never, ever be afraid to talk about your past and your failures. There is nothing more important than blocking the negative attitudes of mean-spirited people.

I thought at one time, "What would I do if I survived testicular cancer?" That got me to think more about time, family, and faith. This book reveals many stories I hid in the crevice of my mind. I want to take you with me through those early cancer days of self-discovery, through nostalgic days, and through my passions and my life's validation. Many of my stories will make you feel and think about your life and purpose, too. If you're interested in coming along for this trip, hop on board. All these mentioned adventures make for good stories. Let's get to them.

That warm September morning in 1981, I stood face-to-face with my own mortality, and I didn't especially like the feeling of being on the wrong side of the grass. As a young man, I thought, *This is it. It is terminal. I am finished—next is "pushing up daisies."*

My cancer diagnosis changed something in me. I started to really see the whole picture and feel like I wanted to make every life moment count. I no longer wanted to fritter away time.

I grew up in an Italian German community. It was a quaint farming and industrial town with very friendly people and great restaurants. As a Midwest boy, I'm still partial to those places where you can find good fried chicken, tenderloin sandwiches, and deep-dish pizza.

I enjoyed running and biking long distances in those days prior to cancer. My friends and I enjoyed the local nightlife as well. We always found amazing bands or DJs playing great '80s music. And the optimal way to beat the heat when I was in my teens was sitting pretty at the local pool while splashing girls, enjoying the hot summer vibe.

1

BEFORE THE DISCOVERY

I was in sixth grade when I realized running was going to be my jam. During a 600-meter competition in gym class, my team beat out more than 300 boys from three different grades. I still remember that competition as if it were yesterday. That feeling of heading into the unknown, the initial feeling of hesitation, then, bang! You're on your way. I hit my stride, my limbs loose with excitement and my pulse beating quickly.

This turned out to be where the real action was. Everything was off the charts, my senses were buzzing, I was alive, in the zone. After I heard the words "On your mark," I lost control. I can still close my eyes and retrace that race from start to finish, every inch of it. That was the beginning of understanding the relationship between hard work and winning.

The head coach encouraged me to go out for the track team when I was in junior high. He saw me run in gym class and knew that I had room for improvement. While running junior high track, I learned there was a direct relationship between hard work and winning races. I liked winning races and improving each meet.

Hearing the bang of the pistol makes me feel sentimental for those days of track. "Runners! Take your marks!" The shot of the gun caused a switch to be flipped; the negative thoughts in my head vanished. The thrill of the race and my competitive spirit reminded me of why I wanted to showcase my natural talents.

I had a constant, looming sense of nervousness and butterflies before my running events. In all other team sports, you have minutes to play, quarters, or innings. If you make a few mistakes, you have time to make up for them, or the coach calls for a timeout. But in the sport of track, you have one shot to get it right. It's a solitary thing that takes a tremendous amount of technique and strategy to master. It can't be compared to another sport.

During my sophomore year in high school, the track and cross-country team coaches convinced me to join. Once I was on the team, I felt a part of something that was bigger than normal life. Every time I began a run, a conversation in my head would start. There can only be one first competition. It is unique and special and is to be treasured. As one competitor at a local 10K said, "It is not so much the challenge, but it is how we overcome weakness. As runners, we train, we push our bodies, but do we perceive the race like going through life itself?"

After I was diagnosed with testicular cancer, a storm was brewing in my life that could have destroyed my future. To combat this, I would dream of running in a secluded spot in nature. It was so enchanting, with a beautiful waterfall, on a path that led me deep into a forest known only to a select few. Was I searching for Nirvana? Had a promise in the back of my mind been resurrected?

Cancer was not to be the end of the road for me. I've since competed in hundreds of races. Yet, that very first was definitely the best. It won over my heart. Now but a distant memory, I still love remembering that race day. It's really simple: I was taken into a future path to be treasured. Thank God for the first time.

Coach Mac

My high school cross-country coach, Mac, held a treasure trove of inspiration and creative thoughts. He encouraged me to embrace curiosity and trust my initial instincts. I learned from him how to dance around fear with a willing mind. Mac taught me to be resilient and fearless when competing against other runners. That creativity still resides within me today.

Mac died suddenly the summer before my junior year, during one of the hottest months in recent summers. In that heat, and with the weight of humid air, came the dissipation of my motivation. I was weak and struggled with focus and time.

It was difficult getting back to the normality that I once had. Hours of running, planned sleep, and a regular routine had created a habit of being alone. The benefits of solitude helped with depression and discovery. But losing Mac was so painful, and I needed to figure out what to do for the best support moving forward.

Without Mac's presence in my life, I remember thinking my life was crashing down. His wisdom had introduced me to a magical adventure. I am proud of those years pursuing my dreams of being a better runner. After my high school career was over, I looked back at myself and was able to embrace the lessons from those Mac years.

Mac often said, "You may not understand this perplexed world today, but someday, wherever you are, you will be grateful for all those things that didn't go quite your way."

Oh, how his way of weaving stories with courage and authenticity helped shape me into the person I am today. I deeply miss him and am grateful to him for being tough on me.

I still wonder what his thoughts would have been upon hearing that I had testicular cancer.

What About Tomorrow?

Before cancer, one day, friends of mine asked me what I wanted to do the next day. I said, "Well, just live." Little did I know that moment in my life would turn out to be one of the most prophetic. That night, I was out at a local pub with a college cross-country teammate, listening to a local band. My teammate and I looked at each other when the band took a break, and we both had the same thought. "Why are we here and not out for a training night run?"

We drove back to my house, changed into shorts and running gear, and set off at 12:30 a.m. on that sultry, hot August night for our training run. We made these kinds of rash shifts all the time. The irresponsible decisions I made in my twenties do not fly when you're thirty-five.

Well, I am an adult now. I do adult things. Every morning, I brew my coffee, put on my favorite walking shoes, tune into my favorite radio station, and grab my newspaper before heading out for a walk. Being patient is not for the impatient, and in those days, I was very impatient, which is why running was a good discipline for me.

Growing up and learning about life demands patience and discipline. Being diagnosed with cancer made me grow up fast.

But I did come back from testicular cancer. Only a few select people really knew how difficult it was for me. While I did not have chemo, I experienced stress, depression, and plenty of wild thoughts. It was rough, and it took multiple decades for me to even begin to feel like life was sustainable.

A Second Chance Wake-Up Call

This story happened months before my cancer diagnosis. After this experience, I allowed myself time to rest and be more emotional and introspective about my well-being.

Second Chance was an under-21 nightclub in Peoria, Illinois. Every Sunday night, we would dance the night away. Many different worlds were suspended in those nights. We parked in the back large gravel parking lot, adjusted our hair, and sprayed a dash of cologne to start the night.

The twenty-five-year-old DJ, a guy named Spinner, was standing in the booth. For the club's "Teen Sunday" night, he was playing "Stayin' Alive" by the Bee Gees. It was a hot, steamy Sunday night, but we went down to the crowded dance floor anyway. My friends and I had certain girls we would dance with weekly. I had two or three I referred to as regulars. If one of my regulars was dancing with someone else, I would ask a random lonely girl who was just gazing at the dance floor and wishing someone would come up and ask them. That was what we liked about the Chance; there was no pressure, just a lot of fun.

In the career-confused generation, one thing everyone under the age of twenty-five definitely wanted was a good-paying job, so we could continue to drive nice cars and date women. When the night was over, my friends and I walked out, got into our cars after asking one another how many telephone numbers we'd gotten that night.

We had bets on these nights. I asked my best friend, Joe, "Do you really want to know?"

"You might as well tell me," Joe said. "I have a pretty good hunch."

That night, I had collected twelve numbers. I wanted those nights to never end. It was the 1980s—a quite simple period, albeit a bit raw at times, and we were just kids.

Oh, there were so many ways to tell our story, the dancing, the number of girls I would never call back. It wasn't like I didn't want to call them. I just got caught up with friends and schoolwork and didn't have a care in the world. We were forever set in that idealized early-MTV decade, where the class-conscious system ruled cultural life, when it was acceptable to spend evenings at dance clubs, interrupting our lives of leisure to chill out in a place of excess.

We have long since said goodbye to that environment of smelly smoke, scary bars, and complicated pickup lines. Many nights of parties, dancing, and more dancing, sometimes late into the evening. Always singing along to many 1980s classic tunes. Driving to the next club in a packed car.

Thinking back, it reminds me that some of my best moments are ones that came from processing the changes in life on the dance floor. Thankfully, my friends and I broke out of that pattern when it no longer suited us.

This particular, typical Second Chance night turned into an unexpected spectacle. It was a muggy July night, and I had driven because I wanted to get home early for work the next morning. I navigated the dark two-lane road at 12:45 a.m. with the radio blasting.

That night, I think the many hours of dancing and becoming all hot and sweaty caused me to doze off. I don't remember nodding off or the flashing lights; however, I do remember my car flipping in midair after hitting a drainage culvert. I remember hearing the sound of crashing metal... and then silence.

My overturned car was smoking from the dust in the field. When I came to, I didn't know how long I had been there pinned upside down, without any water and hardly enough oxygen. Then I heard words being spoken as though someone was right outside the car. Just as I started praying Hail Marys, I heard two voices saying my name and talking to me about remaining calm. Could the angels have been sending me a message?

This got my attention because my name is such a strong part of who I am. Where, after midnight on a Sunday morning, would anyone find me and use my name? Those voices when there was no one around—they had to be angels. This was a chance at redemption. Ironically, that was the name of the club I'd been at hours before the wreck: Second Chance.

Several hometown officers arrived, and an ambulance crew pried open the driver's side door. When I was outside of the car, I asked about the couple who had been talking to me. They looked puzzled and said, "No one else is around."

Tired and hardly able to keep my eyes open, I was disoriented as the dust settled around my car. How does one's car cross the center lane at sixty miles per hour, hit an embankment, flip five yards in midair, land upside down in a cornfield—and live? When I think about that night, my mind somehow produces two words: lost soul.

What I learned from this was that nothing good ever happens after midnight. I wasn't wearing a seatbelt; it wasn't a law back then. Was this all a precursor to a sign that my life was about to change?

I would soon devote huge amounts of time to discovering my life. These endeavors were reflected in the ways in which I interacted with others. A positive life and no looking back were my new mantras. My redemption was that I wasn't a cat with nine lives, yet in the midst of it all, this meant I could make a difference.

2

RELIEF AND A LIFE UNTESTED

Sometimes life just happens. I had a grand childhood; I played hard and experienced many things—just a young boy full of piss and vinegar. From puppy love and breaking school records to the unexpected loss of a much-loved track coach in high school, and a new chapter of life without him.

In the midst of this, I started thinking about the bigger picture. My friends and I had lived life as if it would never end; now it was time to think about what it all meant. I began spending a few minutes a day thinking about what I might want to become. This helped to put things in a new perspective. I dreamt of setting myself up for success and having the confidence to be my best.

Up until that point, I had no complaints at all about life. In fact, after high school graduation, I was pretty happy. I had several offers for track scholarships. I decided to stay local and attend a junior college, where I ran on the cross-country team. But life happened suddenly and took the wind right out of my sails. It was all gone in one small, innocent, chilled morning. It was the day of the state meet for the Illinois Junior College cross-country team.

After the meet, when we didn't qualify for nationals, I went home, took a long, hot shower, and thought about my future. But it was that afternoon that I discovered something so terrible, so mind-bending that it changed my life forever. Circumstances would force me to start a new phase of my life. In the shower that brisk fall day, something was off. I didn't feel right, there was some kind of lump, and I experienced excruciating pain in one of my testicles.

When my dad came in from mowing lawns, I walked downstairs and said, "Dad, I think something doesn't feel right." I told him about the lump, and he said, "Let's get in the car and go to the doctor right now." We headed for our family doctor's office.

He examined me and said, "You need to see a urologist—stat." And within an hour, I was in a urologist's office for an emergency visit.

Dr. K., a short, stocky man with wire-rimmed glasses and an enviable thick head of hair, came in to examine me. He shut the lights off and shone a flashlight on one side of my scrotum. He saw something that concerned him. The next thing I knew, within twenty-four hours, I had an MRI and a sonogram. I was wheeled into surgery for what seemed like an eternity to me.

It Still Haunts Me

"I'm sorry, I have good news and some bad news," Dr. K. said. What happened next still haunts me three decades later. He told me that it had been necessary to remove one of my testicles.

Lying there in Pekin Memorial Hospital in Pekin, Illinois, grief shot through me like a lightning bolt. I'm a young man with my full life ahead of me. This seems so unfair, I thought. I lashed out and hit the handrail hard, nearly pulling out the IV in my arm.

This immediately began a time of questioning, of wrestling with my faith and God. Even more than dealing with the reality of the disease, I was concerned about all the insensitive testicle jokes I'd be subjected to. I heard myself screaming in a high-pitched voice that progressed to a mournful wail. I must have looked as if I had been hit in the face with a sledgehammer.

Through my cancer experience, I learned how to be grateful for both the small things and the big things. I learned not to sweat the bad things and instead live for the good things. I am a more positive person because of what I went through.

Time froze when I heard the news, and I immediately realized I had to make a decision. I could either continue to freak out, or I could put on my Nike waffle trainers and get through rehab before heading back to pound the pavement as a runner. Envisioning running again made me decide I wanted to live.

Strangely, my body vibrated like an electric shock when Dr. K. mentioned the word cancer. I was utterly shocked because I didn't have any symptoms or warning signs. Suddenly, it was as though a frog in my throat was about to jump out. I was terrified. I didn't know how to communicate this news to my extended circles of support.

I knew, though, that I didn't want to die from cancer, like so many millions of others do. They work in offices, travel around the world, and raise children until some shocking news takes place. After a doctor's visit for what seems like a common illness, they're told of a spot, lump, or area that may become dangerous if not treated.

Bracing for Impact

Conversation isn't easy when you're completely naked from the waist down. I stared up at the ceiling tiles, bracing for the impact of the inevitable prognosis. I tried to make sense of the anguish and despair that had been handed to me.

A voice, like a chanting sound at benediction, awakened me. Dr. K. handed me a mirror. "There's no easy way of saying this: a testicular tumor was in you and now is out." An echo and a whisper, like a mortar shell shrieking through my groin, resonated in my head.

The cold hospital gown shocked me into reality. I thought about how wasteful the years of hard work in school and my part-time jobs now seemed. My haunches groaned as I allowed my fingers to feel the loss of my testicle. Dark thoughts and humiliation remained. I knew that testicular cancer was rare. Was this the beginning of the end—or a dark warning for the future? Was I being rewarded by surviving the operation? Was this all a dream? Could all this be a false alarm? I told myself with a tinge of anxiety, *This too will pass.*

No amount of feeling depressed, anxious, or worried would make it all go away. Dr. K.'s words confirmed that the worst had passed: The tumor was gone; I had survived. Profuse tears and prayers welled up in me. I built up the courage to ask in a whisper, "Doctor, what happened to me?"

I felt the marvel of being alive, but I wondered at what price. My guilt of surviving washed over me. The world did not see my scars or feel my pain; it only saw what I allowed to be seen. Like a jigsaw puzzle, that time in my life was very confusing.

I overheard Dr. K. say to an associate, "So many things could have happened; this was a tumor, but there was no spreading of the cancer." One of my biggest concerns was the possibility of never having children. At the time, I was also unsure if I would ever be able to race again.

A Jew Saved My Life

I recently caught up with an old high school friend who'd remembered that a Jewish doctor had saved my life. Growing up Catholic, I always thought the Jews were the chosen ones. After all, I saw *Chariots of Fire*, so it must've been true. Most of us have a core faith in something. It lies in one's mind, a kind of realm of spiritual experiences one remembers.

After my surgery, I encountered these beliefs but never really took them to heart. I have always been a person of belief and faith in taking care of myself. But now, the realization of what is, and a resonating, deep, transcending worship touched my very essence. I questioned if it was the energy of my perfectionism or a connection with an inspired life. After many morning runs, I would ponder and think, *What about the rest of the day? Will there be silence? Will there be something profound that changes my life through the lows and the highs?*

Girls, dating, breakups, they were all just formalities. My life was really going well, but sometimes I would think, *Do having friends or making a lot of money mean that much?* Because what truly means something in the long run is your health. If you have good health, you have everything.

Back in the early 1980s, I was constantly thinking about my past and worrying about my future. Dr. K. taught me to enjoy the small things in life. He planted the seeds, and it took me more than a decade to learn how to be more mindful and appreciate my life. It finally sank in and helped me reduce the stress and anxiety.

I am eternally grateful to Dr. K. for saving the life of this skinny Catholic boy. I experienced nothing less than a prophetic encounter after my surgery. The basic principle in Jewish law states that human life comes first. I also learned that almost any sacred commandment can be broken in order to save a human being's life. I'll never forget that day when Dr. K. performed what many consider a routine procedure.

When I woke up from the anesthesia, I felt euphoria, like a tingling sensation. It was the kind of feeling you get when you have completed something in your life, when you realize you have qualified for something, gotten an A on that college thesis, or gotten the job you never thought you would get. It was Dr. K.'s miraculous, God-given talent that saved my life, and I will always be grateful. That day, my Jewish doctor gave me a second chance and a new look at life.

What Next?

After the cancer diagnosis, I didn't have a clue what I could do with my life, or even what I wanted to do. Some things, by definition, I could resist. I could begin again, but why would I want to? What was my purpose in this life? What would success mean to me in the future? As these questions swirled about in my mind, I knew it was time to change my mindset. During my hospital stay, I had a conversation with a nurse who told me, "Commit yourself to something that will make you happy, something you can be successful at."

I had dreams, and I needed to get on with them. I wondered if the operation would define my future. Would I run with the wind, have the chance to go to college, and meet new people? As a twenty-year-old man with life and a future ahead, having cancer in the picture was terrifying.

There were many practical implications I thought I needed to prepare for—such as to whom would I leave my few prized possessions and trophies if I didn't survive? I pondered my financial readiness as though I had to ensure that my nonexistent children would remember me. *Oh my gosh, I'll never have a wife!* I would suddenly think. *Who will have control over all my assets?* I wanted so much to be the best version of myself.

Preparing for the unknown was the most nerve-wracking, head-banging, and soul-searching experience I'd ever had. I was jumping on this roller coaster and scared to my bones. Adrenaline fueled my tightening muscles with a "punch to the gut" feeling. I waited with bated breath for my first test results to come back and wondered how I could bring myself to call my friends to let them know what had happened.

Now, decades later, I'm back in Pekin visiting many of those friends. This is my town. It's beautiful here, and yet still painful remembering those early days after hearing the "C-word." However, the comfort and support I received from my family and friends was so life-affirming and positive.

Water and Running Saved My Life

Back when I was in school, life was simpler. There was no talk of cancer among young people. I assumed cancer was something that much older people got. It wasn't something a twenty-year-old cross-country college athlete should have. I've since realized that cancer does not care about age.

It was a Saturday post-lunch shower in September that started this whole journey.

What if I hadn't gone for a run that day? What if I hadn't been a runner? What if I were just a "regular Joe"—would I have discovered it when I did? I often think of my dad saying, "Don't use all the hot water." However, as it turns out, being a student-athlete and taking three showers a day did save me. Water has both physical and psychological benefits. It gives one a sense of peace and stimulates the mind. And as it turns out, it was hot water running across my body that helped me discover the tumor.

I was suddenly thrust into uncharted territory, questioning everything I thought I knew about the world, the universe, and myself.

That September day, I had pushed myself to the limit, and looking back, that seems to have been my salvation of sorts. I clearly remember the life-changing moment when fear, stress, and anger all came together. I had contemplated never achieving my goals, but I changed my mind and accomplished them. I've learned that you have to tell yourself that you get what you want through trial by fire.

Water was my saving grace. The shower was my safe space. It was a place where I could leave my worries behind. Running a hot shower helped me cope with whatever I was stressed about at the time.

It is no secret that water provides us with more energy and better health. Not only drinking water, but actually submersing your body in water can totally invigorate your mind. A hot shower made my muscles feel relaxed, and the increased blood flow caused me to be more alert throughout the day.

A warm shower was one of my simple pleasures. Taking that time to unwind and not worry about life for a while. Water is life, and God gave us life. Here in the United States, water is so common that many of us take it for granted, but it is essential to our existence. Water has indeed saved my life, and for that I am eternally grateful.

Over my lifetime, I have come to know that water has healing powers, as many religious people believe. Water supports the body, mind, and soul. Water is something that binds us all together.

When I feel low, water is the thing that cleanses me like an energy field. In an often unpleasant and cruel world, it was the immense clarity and peace of water running down my body that sustained me. It was less about what it took from me and more about what it gave back. With everything that had been going on in my life, water held an intention for me.

My War on Testicular Cancer

When we talk about the war on cancer, more emphasis needs to be placed on the patient and supporting their health and well-being rather than just talking about the actual cancer. *How did I get testicular cancer? Was it something I ate or drank?* There was no history of cancer whatsoever in my family. Was it just the luck of the draw?

I try every day to understand "why me" in the context of the world. As time has gone on, memories of things I regretted doing are now all but a fading story. It was like a war inside my head instead of my body. My overall appearance was particularly good after a large amount of time working on myself. However, there were those days when my life consisted of daily tears. It was a process of realizing that my life was more than just the past.

I have been told repeatedly to refrain from dwelling on the past. I can't change it because whatever has happened has passed and never will return. Coach Mac once told me, "It comes with the territory." He believed that the past was behind us, and even if you failed, you should never regret it. Our failures make us better runners. What we have are memories, and we can cherish them. After all, cancer formed the new me, and I can say now that it's made for a great life.

Running to me was a lifeline. It connected me to individuals and their emotions, and it gave me a sense of purpose in life. It became an outlet for hiding my pain through all the tests and stress. In the midst of my own darkness, I felt empowered to navigate my true feelings.

By running faster than ever before, I could achieve my goal of doing my first marathon. Many local runners suggested that I just aim to finish the race, but I'm not a "just finish it" kind of guy.

I Was Not Born with Testicular Cancer

When they cut my umbilical cord, did the doctor ask, "Do you want testicular cancer?" I think not. I was a baby and had no choice in the matter. However, I choose to believe that what happened to me made me realize how precious my life was, and it also helped me to feel empathy with those who suffer from illness.

In my conversations with my former self, I envisioned a life that wasn't standing still, but evolving, full of happy-go-lucky moments as time went on and dreams gained strength and confidence. Before my cancer, I had a day-to-day routine. Nothing out of the ordinary and remarkably simple. After my cancer diagnosis, I realized how fragile life is. As a competitive runner, biker, and avid outdoors person, I took for granted all that I was able to do.

During my cancer experience, it was important for me to continue hanging out with my good friends. Discovering my use of personal space led to a new discovery. About twice a week, without telling anyone, I would drive to the park and spend an hour or two swinging. Yes, swinging back and forth, back and forth. Somehow, this helped me feel and know, from within, what was truly important.

It was my way of trying to fit in and gain a sense of control. Everyone from urologists and patients to concerned individuals needs to hear this. Having one's sense of control helps in the healing, mental health, and recovery process for all cancer survivors and patients.

I have no issue with people who want to hold their cancer diagnosis as close to themselves as they would a million-dollar winning poker hand. In the end, if someone has the misfortune to have cancer, they should be able to share it any way they want. At one time or another, we're all being watched, critiqued, and analyzed.

I'm tired of hearing people who think they know everything about cancer. I'm a survivor; I'm not fake. Nothing hurts more or screams louder than someone saying something about your current self. I've learned that people will hurt you with their words and their supposed knowledge, and not even think about it.

Truth is what heals. I never had a darker side. There's no myth; there's no story other than this. I am just myself. What I share is for the world; it's not to go on and on about my own losses.

Some days I want to throw a party and announce, "My cancer is gone!" This feels like both a sound statement and a great celebration. No musical accompaniment, no marching bands—just an inspiring makeover.

Embracing a New Way of Life After Cancer

If cancer can happen to me, it can happen to anyone. Now, as a survivor, I want to tell my story and help others in their journey.

These days, I have a very regimented daily schedule consisting of three to four hours of writing, walking on the beach, and a five-day-a-week sauna routine.

You might think of a person with cancer as an unhealthy person with a particular look of yellowish skin, dark circles under their eyes, and a caved-in face. But not all health is physically seen. Some is mental. After my cancer surgery, my life spun out of control with an all gas, no brakes attitude. I became uncertain about my life path. There was no map or instruction book. *How would I navigate life?*

Keeping my mind stimulated was particularly valuable. Actually, taking college classes that played to my personality and that I enjoyed, instead of taking what I thought would look good on a transcript, helped me develop a genuine interest in studying. I began to find my way after many years of tests and follow-up procedures.

Taking interesting courses kept my mind from wandering and focusing on unhealthy behaviors. Behavior and habits are important. My mom knew how hard it was on me as a young man to be sick. In the spring, she would say, "It's a beautiful day for a run." This encouraged me, and I was fearless, diving headfirst into the fray. I tried to run every day and beat my time or distance, even if it was just by a small amount.

Running competitively was my new thing. It helped me shape who I was meant to be. Those race days, even years after my cancer, brought me to a magical place. On race day, all my stress and anxiety would disappear. I was free once that starter shot the gun, and everything that weighed heavily on my mind no longer mattered. Each race day was a celebration.

I trained weekly with a local running group. I trained for six months in preparation for my first marathon. That meant running a total of fifty to sixty miles a week, through pain, rain, and wind. I struggled every day when I thought about my past and future. Some days it was like a cold, hard truth slapping me in the face, much like the winter chill on a December morn. The grim truth is that to be successful in a marathon, one must accept the distance and respect it. Finishing was a signal to me and to the rest of the world that I was not only tough but also recovered.

Reimagining and feeling inspired by the promise of a new way of life, I saw the world differently after cancer. I saw things like stars colliding. I could see myself growing older and becoming more educated about my health. I'd been given the opportunity to have a second life. I questioned my existence and sought answers to my questions.

Here I am today, still alive, and now writing daily about my experiences of surviving testicular cancer and standing tall. No longer the wise guy I was in my youth, my writing has shown me what's possible; it has transformed my life. I have discovered that my words can help others with their cancer survivorship. All of our hopes, dreams, and experiences are like fingerprints in a maze of life. No one else can do this but you. Whether you're a runner, writer, or weekend warrior playing golf or tennis, each story is as unique as a fingerprint.

One must get out of one's four walls once in a while. I have realized that doing new things challenges your mind. It can become too easy to sit at your desk and forget to really live. When you're unsure of your future, you may feel driven to break up the dullness. Action and change are fresh ways of calming your fears. Trying to achieve the right amount of change to calm the mind and grow is exciting.

Losing a Testicle

My experience of cancer was a lonely journey and quite taxing, both physically and emotionally. The effect of losing my testicle, while visibly unnoticeable to others, was very traumatic. A part of me was no longer there. It might as well have been my leg or arm.

Then there were those who offered their opinions about the removal of a testicle. Several told me I would have significantly low levels of sperm production. What? Were they all doctors? Had they studied testicular cancer? No, they were fellow runners who had heard things by talking to people secondhand. Horrible rumors spread throughout my local running community.

Everyone had a story, usually beginning with the statement that they knew someone who had a testicle removed. They were told their sperm would be low. Why was everyone so concerned about my personal love life or sex life? They were just busybodies with nothing else to talk about.

The absence of a testicle was not only significant to twenty-something me but also had emotional consequences that led to questions in certain social settings. After the removal of my testicle, Dr. K. did warn me that there was the possibility of decreased sperm production. Not knowing what that meant exactly, it still scared me a whole bunch. Many a morning, I would lie in bed pondering whether I would be able to have children someday. Before the surgery, I was not emotional and never thought much about life experiences. Years after my surgery, I could not recognize that voice within. I was looking for an answer, a certain response from a friend, a parent—from anyone, really. I never received it because everybody saw my outward smile and persona as being that everything was OK.

When I lost my testicle, it felt like someone had passed away. No words can really describe how I felt. There was a deep feeling of inadequacy and inner pain. Sometimes I forgot, and then I would suddenly remember that the scar was there. But sometimes I would remind myself that this had been a matter of life and death. This loss was something that had a good ending.

What would I look like when the staples came out and the stomach muscles healed? I'd look like a California coastal roadmap, but it would be a map revealing a life still to live. At one point, my good friend Joe asked me my thoughts on being a survivor. It was simple: **I told him the surgery was so I could live, not just survive.**

I learned something during that period. It was clear that I had a lot on my mind. At times, I wasn't very talkative. Often, I'd respond with just a shrug and a few words. I learned that if I sat quietly and looked distraught, people would pay attention to what I had to say. My mind was agitated over things. The weight of expectation was looming.

Maybe I was ahead of my time. Learning to be quieter at times helped me understand the limitations of my mind. Today, here I am, still alive and standing. No longer a wise guy.

I believe in the impossible. It's transformed my life.

Gleaning Power From Loss

Despite these struggles, I took the positives and thanked my family, friends, and teammates for their support. Looking back at people and places, I reflected on continuity and learning from the past to consider my future. I knew where I had been, but I did not know where I was going.

Cancer opened my eyes to life and to the real future. I was leery to share my experiences during my illness. There was a grief process—I did lose something. I learned about the power and the strength of vulnerability during that time. Cancer was now a part of my life. After my surgery and getting the "all clear" for the cancer not spreading, I struggled for a long time with work, friends, and dating. I immersed myself in partying to calm my anxieties. I didn't even realize that's what I was doing at the time.

A local group of runners helped me confront the reality of recovery after surgery. They said, "These circumstances are difficult, but sunny days are ahead of you. Quit thinking and get your focus on running." The shadow of surgery vanished, and courage and new challenges prevailed. I was not accustomed to dealing with the sudden feeling of loss. A positive attitude and survival felt more heroic, but my feelings changed daily, hourly, or even minute by minute.

I did go back to running. I learned to accept the loss, determined not only to survive, but also to thrive. I also realized that some of my work was good enough for prime time. I read every day until my eyes hurt. Then I decided to step outside the rough and tough world we now live in and get my Master of Fine Arts (MFA) in creative writing. At Lindenwood University in Saint Charles, Missouri, I learned to express my joys and insecurities through writing, which helped me to overcome my past.

Road Races After Cancer

The convergence of race participants from the local population included international students from across the pond. During the short season, males and females met every Saturday or Sunday to compete against one another for prizes and set personal records. On race day, all my stress and anxiety would disappear. I was free once the starter shot that pistol. Everything that didn't matter would wash away.

Each race day was a celebration. After all, I was sharing my hopes and dreams on the course. As a competitor, I know strange things happen in races. I look at the places where my life diverges from "normalcy." That is where my story begins.

It's a funny thing about life after cancer—nothing is better than being able to forget about your past. In my case, my past was those sad endless summer nights after my surgery. I was struggling. At times, my brain seemed to shut down, and I was unable to receive any kind of advice. Sometimes I needed time to recover. Sometimes I gained strength in sharing inspirational stories of people who have helped me through this difficult journey.

Those simpler times, running with no worries, made me ready to find my way back to them. I didn't yet realize that involvement in my treatment would require even more from me. In the end, I would discover myself and the world that was to be grand.

My morning moods, at times glum, faded over time. This journey felt more like an exhausting routine, and I would rather stop and eat grass than keep going. The truth was that my personal zest had dwindled, but my motivation had been renewed. If a stranger were to ask me what the most important steps in my running path were, I'd go back to efficiency. Set lofty goals and increase pace. Be me.

I would think back to my high school track and cross-country days when my co-captain, Pacer, always made me work harder and think stronger. Coach Mac continuously talked to us about the struggles, the journey, and the victories. We weren't perfect, and we knew it, but we prevailed as best we could.

As teenagers, Coach Mac had a powerful presence in our lives. He inspired us to persevere, to overcome life's obstacles. We pushed through losses and hard practices. He ingrained in us not to back down. The competition was fierce. We all accepted that it was a reality we'd have to face and overcome.

My spark of motivation in my training regimen was to commit to five miles. It might seem a trivial amount, but it was a worthy start. Those five miles were my first strides on this creative marathon. As I got into the groove, I extended my sprints; a runner still building his stamina.

3

MORE TO CONSIDER

D r. K. took the stethoscope out of his ears and placed it on the bed in his examining room. "Everything looks OK," he said as I sat up. Then he looked at me with his soft brown eyes and said, "Before this surgery, there was nothing really to worry about. Now, this experience is part of your new form; you've come a long way from when I first met you."

Dr. K. and I had some tough conversations. He believed it was important to be upfront, honest, and pragmatic with his patients. What separated him from the rest of the pack was how kind he was. He patiently listened to a young man's crazy thoughts about his own body and life. He took the time to ask how I was doing emotionally, extending a comforting touch. I was alone, but Dr. K. made me feel that we were in it together.

What frightened me most was the thought of losing my voice. What would happen to me if I were not a trailblazer? After all, I had hopes of meeting the woman of my dreams and having a family someday. What would my chances be now that I had only one testicle? What would happen if I didn't meet someone who would accept me? No one ever said, "Did you ever think about freezing your sperm?" As a twenty-one-year-old, things were difficult enough without having something like that hanging over my head. As I reflect back now, freezing my sperm truly would have been a thorny issue—was it the right thing for a young Catholic guy? After all, procreation should be natural. But since no one broached the subject with me, it ended up being a non-issue.

I was lucky to have a cancer that has a very high cure rate. I had been declared cancer-free after two surgeries and an intense amount of testing. Having cancer has changed my life and led to an enduring but even more unsettling path to discover life's challenges and much more.

1:00 a.m. Before the Lymphangiogram

At 1:00 a.m., the sixth floor was quiet, with its cold tile floors and bright lights flickering off the ceiling from pumps and monitors in the various patient-occupied rooms. I dozed uncomfortably in an unfamiliar hospital bed; my legs were weak from the previous morning's surgery, when they had twisted and contorted my body. The industrial blankets smelled like chemicals and were not soft.

"What time is the lymphangiogram procedure tomorrow?" I asked one of the night nurses. I had no idea what a lymphangiogram was, but it sounded horrible. I paused and almost swallowed my tongue, thinking of another horrific procedure.

"I'm not sure," the husky nurse said. "I can try to find out for you, though."

I looked down at the gown covering my skinny runner legs. They looked like something between a roadrunner and a rubber chicken. Would I ever run again, or ever feel that runner's high on a summer morning with the dew coming off the lawns and the streets empty? I would look back and realize that if I turned my head, I was still the same person. I still may have been skinny, but I wasn't taking a back seat to anyone.

I lived that little fact of humanity amid all the dire results and grim prognostics. As a male in my early twenties, I had plenty of normal insecurities and fears. I was also carefree and tended to trust everyone. That feeling of innocence helped my understanding of why such sad things happened and helped me find ways to rid myself of trauma in the future.

I never thought that simple pleasures like ice cream on a summer day, popcorn at the movies, and a date with a high school sweetheart would be something that I would cherish for life. My problems, fears, and insecurities would all leave. No promises that they would never come back again.

I knew there was a possibility that the lymphangiogram would show that the cancer had spread to my lymph nodes. Would that lymphangiogram save me? I realized that paying attention to myself was what I needed to focus on. Focusing on anything else would not be beneficial.

Getting back to living was what I needed to do. There were no products to diagnose, treat, cure, or prevent any testicular cancer. Thus, I couldn't make any kind of predictions at this point in my life. All I could do was hope for the best and prepare for the future. It was an uneasy discovery.

I wish I knew more about the lymphangiogram. The dye was uncomfortable and caused a mild burning sensation in my legs. My foot and calf turned a Smurf blue. That color remained for about 8 weeks before slowly fading. Friends and family joked that I was trying out for a cartoon movie.

The Proctoscopy

I asked the gastroenterologist about the proctoscopy. The young doctor, who was maybe forty-years-old, said, "Well, son, it's so you're protected against getting any secondary cancer."

Secondary cancer? What?

"As a survivor, you have a higher chance of developing a new cancer outside the testicle that was removed," he explained. This could mean bladder, kidney, and rectal cancers. Dr. K. felt obliged to take measures to prevent a recurrence.

The procedure took about twenty minutes. As a patient with testicular cancer, I was first evaluated by physical exams and many procedures, including chest X-rays, abdominal X-rays, blood and kidney scans, an MRI, and a CAT scan. It all seemed excessive to a young guy like me. Dr. K. told me that testicular cancer survivors are also at risk for metabolic syndrome, infertility, cardiovascular disease, and psychosocial disorders. The proctoscopy procedure had a shorter operational time and a much lower rate of post-op complications than I would encounter in my treatment.

The proctoscopy was an outpatient procedure. I was up walking and eating within hours of the procedure. Back then, I wasn't given any counseling on the aftereffects or concerns I might have. Of course, today, I'm sure there would be a whole class on the procedure.

I was told at the time they were doing this as a precautionary measure so I could live. So, of course, my parents and I didn't question Dr. K. or the young gastrointestinal surgeon. However, the truth is that I am glad they did the procedure. It eliminated the thought of the presence of any such polyp or abnormal growth while also checking for colorectal cancer.

The proctoscopy involved inserting an endoscope (a tube with a camera on it) into my rectum and colon. It wasn't what I would call a comfortable feeling. I felt something push, and then I felt a rush like I just had a bowel movement. Lying on a cold table in a fetal position wasn't my choice for sure. I had built myself up for the worst, expecting to feel pain when he inserted a gloved, lubricated finger into my rectum to check for any blockages.

Then the young doctor started talking medical gibberish. It might as well have been Chinese because I hadn't a clue what he was saying. I yelled out, "Doc, am I going to live?"

"Yes," he said. "The results of your proctoscopy show nothing abnormal."

Funny how the thought of death can inspire you to live…

Long-Lasting Feelings

Having testicular cancer came with long-lasting feelings of loss and shame. Not only did I have a testicle removed, but I was also suffering a male emotional response to trauma. As I worked my way through this, I learned that everyone is searching for something. Athletes, students, or teachers, we're all searching for the same thing: our place in life, a sense of well-being, and a feeling of contentment.

When people asked how I was feeling about all the tests I'd had, I gave a forthright but positive response. I said that even though I wanted to be done with them, I didn't want to stand in the way of getting the chance to have closure with the cancer. My new feeling of staying more self-aware is the way I am now, but back then, it was not.

Although the cancer wasn't visible in imaging, blood tests indicated that my cancer was not spreading. My adopted persona didn't tell the true story that I was "living a mental nightmare." I was scared, sad, and unpredictable. Friends and family graciously put up with my tantrums.

Once I got the all-clear from Dr. K., I explored different ways to survive. I had almost forgotten that there was more to life than tests and more tests. *Something has to give,* I thought. Life needed to say yes to every whim of mine. After all the cancer months of being poked and prodded, I had forgotten about living my life. But now, the all-clear would be a sign of what was to come. I needed to get serious about life, think about finding a good woman, settling down, and start living.

More than anything, I wanted a meeting with the doctors to hear the words "You're clear– no more tests." I felt that would never come. The feeling that a black cloud was hanging over me was removed. I could now envision a new beginning, a new lease on life. I could be energized after all those years of worrying that cancer might come back. Now I could have the time I always wanted, all the years I should've been living, the years cancer stole from me.

The Forty-Five Minute Procedure

That forty-five-minute lymphangiogram was all I needed to discover I was cancer-free. My fears went away temporarily when I heard it was prescribed by Dr. K for me. A blue dye, called contrast, would be infused into the webbing between my first and second toes on each foot. Then, a small cut would be made and a tube inserted into the channel.

That was the easy part.

A very rough-and-tumble radiology technician entered my room. "When the lymphangiogram is over, I'll sew up the little cuts," he told me. I figured he would give me some shots in my foot and stitch me up. Instead, he handed me a large white towel and said, "Put this towel in your teeth and bite down. You're going to want to punch, kick, and hit me, but please don't."

What I felt next was a blazing, scorching, torrid fire in my toes. The pain was more excruciating than if I had touched the sun itself. When the doctor asked if I required a cup of ice to chew to help ease the pain, I screamed, "No, please just make it stop!" In total, after the dye was injected, the procedure took less than the length of a Catholic Mass, but it felt like an eternity. I was disoriented, self-conscious, and dizzy.

But it was then that I embarked on a life change, a new beginning. No more feeling sorry for myself, no more melancholy. Although I was afraid of a blank page in my journal and scared of being together with someone of the opposite sex, I was prepared to be more than a survivor. I had my life, a great family, and good friends. God gave me a second chance. The day I was released to go home, I told my doctor I was going to get plenty of rest so I could wake each morning feeling refreshed and ready to run another 5k race. To combat the fear of cancer returning, that's what I would focus on. Focusing on anything else would not be beneficial.

I began to see the world differently. I could see myself growing older and becoming more educated about my health. I'd been given the opportunity to have a second life. This was a joy that aligned with my excitable natural attitude.

Months later, I felt quite well and energized, emotionally and physically. Although I was not going to climb a mountain any time soon, I found myself experiencing the feeling of coming off a ledge. Euphoria came over me like ice-cold water on a 110-degree day. A rush of adrenaline—a life worthy of swimming back up to the top to breathe again.

A Roller Coaster

Nine months after my surgery, Dr. K. advised me that friends and acquaintances would continue to ask or want to hear about my experience. My hometown newspaper wanted to interview me, the local runner and cancer survivor. I wanted to be left alone, or at least just talk about running, not my cancer. My euphoria over having been given a new chance in life gave way to the grind of work, school, and life as a twenty-year-old.

I became overly sensitive, sometimes crying or becoming irrationally angry over insignificant issues. I longed to be happy again. I wondered whether the removal of my testicle caused this effect on my emotions. Specifically, I wondered if emotions and negative thoughts were caused by having less testosterone. Maybe having only one testicle was more of a psychological puzzle than a physical loss.

I experienced each day as if it were the same as in the movie "Groundhog Day." When I got the "all clear" message one year after surgery, my eyes were opened again. Everything was bright. I no longer feared my life changing. Being positive, healthy, and alive were the most important things. I saw an opportunity to be me. I thought, *Why not train for a marathon? At least I might get the feeling of a runner's high.* I started by training for a mile-long race, the Run for Congress.

Run for Congress

In silence, I talk to myself about the boy I had been. People never knew about the gift that changed my life. I have but a few special memories of racing that signify a motivation to my love of running. The summer heatwave, with humidity levels rising, slowed runners' spirits. My skin showed signs of peeling from the sun's harsh rays. The mile-long race, with no water breaks, left runners with muscle cramps, heat exhaustion, and dehydration. You needed to be aware of these issues and stay hydrated.

The runners came in all shapes and sizes, three hundred of them. I was facing the race of my life–for my life, against cancer. A year earlier, I had discovered the malignant tumor in my testicle. Up to that point, I had been healthy and strong; I'd never been a hospital patient in my young life.

After a serious start, I was able to cross the finish line with a time of 4:32.18. I had trained pretty hard, sometimes wondering what I was doing to my body, but I wanted to be able to keep running and keep winning. Dr. K was amazed at the progress I had made. He said, "It's not good–it's fantastic!" He said the operation to remove my testicle and lymph nodes was as serious as open-heart surgery.

During the one-mile race, the crowds were cheering, the runners' feet were stomping, and they were huffing and puffing, grunting like farm animals. It was only 5,280 feet, 63,360 inches, or 1,760 yards. I was guiding through it, block by block; the maze of paces was exhilarating for a young hometown boy. Clad in my Nike racing shoes and athletic gear, I was both scared and nervous during this inaugural open-mile race. I needed to push beyond what I would ordinarily do since my surgery. I had kept myself in pristine running condition since my cancer diagnosis, but I realized my body was sensitive. Some people believe gut-wrenching pain during the race is being human for some period of time. Others know the pain and discomfort are part of the process. It is not done until after the finish line.

The rules were pretty simple. Knowing that I was pushing myself to cross that finish line, I was making a statement for all people who are not yet cancer survivors, as well as those who are. There was also the tension of running at such a great institution as the Everett Dirksen Memorial Library.

During that run, all my senses were heightened. I could see into the future as I crossed the finish line and broke through the tape. My mental awareness was no longer a mystery. I became obsessed with the details of how I would fight off two very fierce competitors. In the end, my main goal, with feet and flurry, led me across the finish line, and I won first place.

I didn't know how good a runner I was until after the Run for Congress. The next day, people all over the area called me and said wonderful things. I went out that night with friends for a drink. As so often happens in the Midwest, a warm day can be followed by frigid temperatures the next day. The temperatures dipped below freezing that evening.

That day ended with me believing that everyone's suffering is real. I have never wanted to look the other way. That one-mile race taught me that whatever I would do in the future, I would build a life outside of what I knew.

Steamboat Classic 15K

My next race, a 15k, took place at 7:00 a.m. on a steamy day in early June. As my high school track coach once said, "Sluga, you first have to know where the trail leads so you know how you're going to get there."

During training, I had mastered the killer hill on the Steamboat 15-kilometer racecourse. One spring night, I announced to our local running club that no one knows everything about running and that we're all still learning. Few of the racers actually knew that I was a testicular cancer survivor.

I paused, cleared my throat, and walked over to the local contingent of runners. Those who knew me gave me encouraging looks. My voice hovered between friendly and stern as I shared that we were all in this together. I said, "The hill before us is a challenge we have to meet. It's the very first step to mastering your own path to victory and success in life."

I had discovered that racing up this hill three times was my impulse to recapture my lost youth. This made me think about the various things people do to improve and become more confident. Those training sessions reminded me that I'm smarter now that my cancer is in the rearview mirror. For those who long for health and contentment, let me stand before you and salute.

Many great runners before me were beaten by "the hill." Everyone agreed that no matter what your skill level was, the neighbors down the street and the onlookers would cheer for you. For one to survive the hill, you must connect to those who have crossed the finish line before you.

The Steamboat Classic 15k has been regarded as the toughest race in the Midwest. It's famous for the hilly loops the racecourse takes in Glen Oak Park. Running up that hill, I imagined myself in someone else's shoes. I found myself turning to the dread of running that hill. One needed to have the proper mentality; it can make a big difference running the Steamboat.

My upper body ached as I leaned into the hill. However, I grew tougher with each physical step. Sweating out my frustration on the hill helped me heal; that's when I began to feel strong. As I came down from that hill the last time, in the back of my mind, I was thinking, *Wow, here I am competing with some of the best 15-kilometer runners in the Midwest. If I can survive losing a testicle and being sliced, prodded, and poked, running three big hills should be a cakewalk.*

I cherished the many words of encouragement from my fellow runners. No matter how much I planned for Steamboat Hill, nothing prepared me for the last few miles. Unless you've gone through it yourself, you won't really understand. It changes you, for better or for worse.

Coming down the hill at mile seven, I saw the blue sky layered against the clouds. At that moment, I could no longer feel my feet touching the ground. For the first time, I felt there was light at the end of my running tunnel. Remembering how much training I had done on that hill, I never imagined that something that hard would be easy on race day. Running that 15k was my escape. It gave me strength at a time when I needed it most. It allowed me to prove to myself that I was capable of far more than I could have ever imagined.

Running races after being a testicular cancer survivor rescued me during some of the hardest times of my life. Times when I wondered if cancer would rear its ugly head and return. Body aches aside, what I've treasured most is that running was good for my post-cancer attitude. It helped me get outside of my head games and live with the spirit and mental health that I needed. The training exhausted me and wore me out, but running is all about the body and what it can do.

After the finish, I thought that Steamboat Hill wasn't so bad. Those miles before and after offered new hope for my racing. But that was only the first of many obstacles to come. Dedication and reverence for myself have always been my passions.

I knew that I needed to vow to keep breathing and keep pushing myself to take the wins and accept the losses. Conquering Steamboat Hill was much like conquering the tumor inside me. That 15k helped broaden my understanding of how to connect to the rest of the runners. That hill was the only thing standing in my way of finishing the race. Those runners lucky to grind out the 9.3-mile race don't often talk about the three strenuous loops with the same hill. It's mentally tough to leave it on the hill as a place where perserverance connects with life.

Marathon Talk

People have been quick to ask me when I discovered I wanted to run a marathon. Did I receive an invitation, have a dream, or was I maybe fishing for a wild pre-marathon beer and pasta-loading story? It didn't happen like that, all at once. I got a feeling for what I wanted, and I went for it. It was different from anything I had ever worked for. Those differences pushed me in a certain direction. But as this story goes, long before I knew a name for it or desire entered the picture, I always loved a challenge. And this was a challenge to complete 26.2 miles. I was never one to back down from a challenge.

It's all from one's perspective. Emotions surrounded me as the concept of completing the marathon lodged in my mind. Conditions are different for everyone. It's a mindset. Many people run away from a challenge that seems like a dream.

Just as businesses rethink their strategies and plan for a new year, longer-term thinking was essential to my game plan. It was going to be a challenging one, but above all, I had my own personal vision. And after my miraculous feat, I went out the next evening and splashed beer and danced like it was my wedding day.

Thinking back to that first marathon, I had to be truly adventurous and willing to chase clouds. It was an emotional recovery. The journey was daunting, but I focused and mastered it. Now, one of my dreams was in the books, and it determined that my personal cancer story had a silver lining.

Running Beats Cancer

Hearing that the great track and field runner Steve Scott had been diagnosed with and survived testicular cancer inspired me. If a superb runner like Scott could return to the track, there was hope for me.

I challenged myself to wake up early every morning for a five-mile run before classes and work. Once or twice a week, I would go for a longer run. When I started training for my first marathon, I trained with my friend Joe. Once he biked alongside me for twenty miles and helped me through the boredom by singing pop tunes and making me laugh.

Running truly was my own personal therapy. I could run and train by myself or with a group of colleagues and friends. Slowly, I began to understand who and what I really was as a survivor.

A running mentor of mine once said, "Sometimes running is the thing we do to make sense of the world." I didn't understand at the time how true that was. Running was just the vessel I needed. It was something that I did that became my rescue, and it had been a long haul to get there. I felt stronger, knowing the testicular cancer was in the past. I was a survivor! Racing was my way of making sense. I could not let losing a testicle control my life.

Many friends and acquaintances in my small hometown often would ask me, "How do you feel?" It felt awkward to say I had a dream, a goal I was willing to work for. It felt even crazier to detail the physical and emotional pain of the past, so instead, I'd shrug my shoulders, and say, "Did I tell you? I'm going to run a marathon!"

The History of the Marathon

I wanted to run a marathon and be inspired by ancient Greek history. The origin of the marathon race dates back to the fifth century. I did my research after getting the all-clear to start running again. I thought if I could train my mind and body to last, I could finish a marathon. Many friends and college mates thought I was crazy. Sally, a cashier at the local Independent Grocers Alliance (IGA) where I worked, said, "Run 26.2 miles in one day?"

It is said that the legendary messenger soldier Pheidippides ran twenty-five miles between Athens and the city of Marathon. His goal was to deliver news of the victory of the battle of Marathon. Pheidippides became a local legend.

That myth actually occurred. In 490 BC, over the course of several days, Pheidippides ran three hundred miles from Athens to Sparta and back to gather additional forces to defend against a Persian attack. The Athenians won the Battle of Marathon days later and then marched twenty-five miles back home from Marathon to defend against a potential second attack.

That march was conflated with Pheidippides' initial run-in retellings of the battle written centuries later, including Robert Browning's 1879 poem "Pheidippides." That myth inspired French archaeologist Michel Breal to propose a similar event for the 1896 Athens Olympics.

The first Olympic marathon featured only seventeen runners traversing a 24.8-mile course between the Marathon battlefield and the city of Athens. Like Pheidippides, I too wanted to run long distances; I wanted to run a marathon. My goal meant pushing through many obstacles and doing what I never thought I could. Completing my first marathon successfully proved that those seemingly insurmountable obstacles were real, and the months and miles were worth the wait. I wanted to race others at distances more than what I raced in high school or college, so I did just that. Training for racing those long distances was liberating.

Still today, whenever I bike or exercise, I remember those times and the closeness I felt to the legendary Pheidippides. What happened centuries ago on the hillsides of ancient Greece helped shape me, a young runner growing up in the Midwest, where people were friendly, wholesome, and had a human desire to make the world a better place.

By participating in several marathons, the physical challenges pushed my limits of performance. My horrible life-changing experience with testicular cancer only emphasized the importance of physical fitness and mental toughness.

My routine was productive and enough every day, no day of rest. Rest is for the weak, I thought. Yet training is never the same for everyone.

As we all do, I've had to move on without the many people and places that have shaped me. It hurts to say goodbye, but I owe it to myself to leave the past behind. Running was my "me time"—on any day, just my two running trainers and the road.

Every day can bring a new stage of life, running enriched me with new insights and experiences from fellow friends and my running community. Training daily was important, and having the ability to share my life with others made me feel grateful. Oh, that crisp fall air as I smelled the fallen leaves! Even feeling my legs hurt helped to set the mood.

After a race, I was approached by a competitor who asked, "Do you mind my asking where you bought your racing tights?" I gave him the details and even told him where he could purchase them.

"Thanks so much. I'll look tonight," he said.

I didn't want to look like everyone else on race day. I bought those tights thinking that the modern Greeks would dress like this. I wore those outlandish running tights before they were in vogue. I still remember the looks I received. It was my first understanding of what it meant to revel in standing out.

Clothing in ancient Greece consisted of linen or wool fabric. Greeks wore light clothes as the climate was hot for most of the year. I figured if Greeks believed in minimal clothing, then I was all about it.

Without knowing it, they were the first influencers of the sports world. They were trendsetters before there was a trend.

Tights improve one's performance and recovery. The actions of fleet-footed messenger Pheidippides inspired the creation of the world's most popular mass participation running race: the marathon. To conclude the story of the marathon, Pheidippides ran without stopping, proclaimed to the citizens of Athens, "We have won," and then died. Pheidippides' last words: "My feet are killing me!"

Throughout history, the marathon has continued to be something people seek to achieve. I wanted to be in that same company. Completing a marathon is a revered goal that, once reached, changes a person's life forever. It not only requires physical fitness, but mental fitness as well.

Running with perseverance, the race marked out, a marathon requires daily discipline and persistence. The marathon is not a sprint; one must stay on the course and remain faithful to the end. Running and faith led me to where I am today. I will never forget that first marathon. Running matters, living matters.

Training With My Buddy Joe

Dr. K. provided the encouragement I needed to stick with running. Then I saw an opportunity to differentiate myself. I thought, *Why not train for a marathon?* The presence of the sacred feeling of a runner's high motivated me. It is what guides the runner and provides the focus of an inspired direction.

Running was my go-to therapy. All my competitors treated me differently after I was cleared to race after my surgery. Everything that I went through back then still lingers today. Cancer was the elephant in the room that no one was talking about. In the years that followed, what I cherished most was compassion for the little things. Life's simple pleasures.

I decided to race my first marathon in another state where no one would know my name. Terre Haute, Indiana, where the marathon was sponsored by Marathon Oil, seemed like a good choice. There were flat cornfields everywhere. I completed the race in just over three hours and thirteen minutes. Next, I set my sights on the Windy City–the Chicago Marathon. This would be a bigger deal, with big crowds and more competition. This time, I would be much more serious about training and preparation.

When I was preparing for my first post-surgery marathon, I came across a unique training plan that involved carb loading. After all, 26.2 miles wasn't a walk in the park. My best friend Joe was Italian, so loading up on pasta sounded like a good plan. For a lover of pizza and everything pasta, like me, this was not going to be hard. I lived by the mantra "Stay the course on race day."

I really did not need imagination, but I did need a shot of adrenaline. I have always believed life is what you make of it, despite all the obstacles. Life doesn't care about your small stuff. When you spend time doing the things you want to do, it's sometimes extremely easy to get distracted by those things that don't really matter.

Through running, I learned to clear my mind of the chaos inside my brain. If I hadn't, I would never have been able to heal my mental state. As I ran mile after mile, years of stress and worrying subsided. I learned to deal with negativity head-on. I devised a scheduling system that would make it easy for me to complete my marathon challenges. Like my training schedule, I needed to eat and sleep much better than I had before I started my quest. So much for those late-night parties and clubs! On a Friday or Saturday night, the place I liked to be was asleep in bed. I was determined that I would never become my own enemy. And after months of running and praying, I was able to set aside fear and go after life.

Training for that first marathon was a new experience. Although amazing, my body and attitude were slightly unnerving; I was completely outside my high school sprinter comfort zone. For my next day solution, I was going to spend some time on detailed thoughts. In the meantime, this was a valuable time in my life. It gave me a lot to think about. I knew all about balancing running, diet, and taking care of my overall well-being. Only twenty months from that dreaded surgery, I was not only a competitive runner but also a cancer survivor.

Joe understood my cancer fight. He got how a diagnosis totally shifted my perspective on life, survival, and what's enormously important. I came up with an idea of how he could help me with my goal. He became part of my training, which was to bike along with me for twenty miles. I had driven the twenty-mile course the night before, stopping to mark the five, ten, and fifteen-mile points with white spray paint. I enjoyed the early morning run the next day with my friend biking alongside me.

This training was when I became a true friend to myself. Joe helped me on that twenty-mile training run to understand how much was riding on this. If I could complete a marathon, if I could conquer the fears and anguish I was feeling every moment of the day, I would not only survive but thrive.

It wasn't my favorite pair of shoes, a beloved running shirt, or even my trusty running shorts that got me through that twenty-mile training run. It was the fact that I had one trusted friend to help me make it through. Through each marathon training run, I could count on being entertained mile after mile by my friend.

Joe would start out easy, full of goofy laughter and conversation. As the run went on, we might touch on more existential topics. But that summer, my running world was about to be shaken. On the magical October morning I was about to run my first marathon, it hit me: I had no one to run with. Joe was out in the crowd cheering me on, no longer keeping me entertained.

What would I do when I hit the wall? To whom would I talk? Who would sing and tell stories like Joe did? So, I did the next best thing. In my head, I sang that favorite song of ours, "Lady." I did it all by myself, and it worked.

I remembered the first time I ran twenty miles with Joe by my side on his ten-speed. Prior to that, I'd never run more than twelve miles at a time. During the second half of that run, at about mile-marker fifteen, my legs felt like lead weights, and my feet were becoming hot and blistered. I felt exhaustion of a much different kind. I was completely drained physically and sapped of mental strength. The muscles in my legs felt totally used up, and they hurt clear to the bone. The last few miles, Joe said, "Come on, come on, Bri. Let's sing!"

Of course, Joe would try to bring me up by singing a song. He picked a song by Little River Band. It was a song that reflected on a past love, along with feelings in the present. I believe that's why he picked that song to sing. The Little River Band lyrics tell a story of the complexities of love. It suggests one should take the time to be present in a relationship and not let one's heart grow cold.

Joe knew I was struggling with dating and relationships since my cancer. He could always analyze my mood by my facial expression. Running was my replacement for expensive therapy. It was how I dealt with my emotions. Sometimes, painful thoughts surfaced of people in the hospital who didn't have the outcome I did. Some days it felt like my entire life was put on hold while I was training for my first marathon.

Joe's singing reminded me of my high school days. My teammates and competitors called me a "musical runner" because I would often listen to music on headphones before track meets, between races, and on team bus rides. Joe's singing on all those training runs was imprinted in my brain, and during the actual marathon, I was able to let that song fill my mind and help me through the rough spots.

Next Up: Windy City Marathon

There I was in my Nike Air Pegasus shoes, the best thing since the Big Mac in my book. I was feeling proud of myself as I stretched out. My singlet with my racing number and running shorts barely covered my body on this cold October morning. As I warmed up for the Chicago Marathon, I couldn't believe that I was going to run another 26.2 miles just twenty-four months after my surgery.

When I started to take running seriously, I built a community, not just consisting of whoever I competed against, but all the sideline runners who were cheering us on. I suddenly had respect for everyone who was out there on a Saturday morning, giving up their precious time.

One thing runners can take away from this marathon training experience is that being a good person is much more important than winning. At this particular race, I began to lose steam and felt myself stumbling just after 26.2 miles, collapsing on the ground after crossing the finish line.

That finish will always be more valuable than being on a podium or being interviewed by someone. I witnessed firsthand how the power of running can positively impact the lives of people on their own journey. I learned more about myself and how to live in the moment. Before the surgery, I tended to live in the past. I thought that was where happiness was supposed to be.

I had put every ounce of my soul into training for this Chicago Marathon. Training for it was the best way to take my mind off the tests and doctor visits. Running had always been my escape, a sanctuary for my heart and mind. Running made me forget the world. It was the repetition and ritual that put me in a good frame of mind.

As I was lining up for the race, I had the feeling of excitement with butterflies in my stomach. I needed to turn those pre-race jitters into routine calmness. I looked through the crowd and saw my parents and Joe. After hearing the starting gun shot, I was off to run the race of my dreams.

Just beginning after mile number six, a huge tremor shook my body; I sucked in air, rose up, and examined what was coming down the road before me. A faint patter of running shoes clopping on the hard pavement rose from the distant street to the high-rise towers. My perception melted into silence, broken only by the creak of the wheelchair's entrants. The cadence of feet from behind them sounded like a herd of buffalo.

I passed a young guy in his thirties in a low-rider wheelchair, a special racing bike. He gave me a thumbs up. I turned to him and said, "Keep the faith." I'll never forget that guy. Here I was running, sweating, and feeling like I was the only one with troubles. Lo and behold, this guy had a physical disability that kept him from running, and he was encouraging me, a guy with perfect legs. Talk about a humbling life moment.

I was pushing myself as hard as I could. At mile ten, I muttered to myself, "Has cancer changed me?" I didn't know that by running a marathon I would sort my life out. I listened to loud music playing all along the race route. I had very deep, soul-searching dialogues with myself throughout the entire race. Along the race route, I remember seeing posters protesting the Iran-Contra scandal and high unemployment. Reaching the twenty-mile mark, my mind wandered, but always came back because I had a purpose and a destination. It was important to take a moment and remember how hard I worked to get to this point. Running for time, and also competing against myself, I realized that what I had been missing was that sense of community, especially being with friends and family.

I crossed the finish line in just over three hours. Those three hours produced blisters and a dehydrated body. My feet, the feet that had endured the lymphangiogram, had taken me 26.2 miles and ensured I met my dream of finishing the race.

Fourteen months prior, my hospital room was near a garden in the south courtyard. I would sneak out in the morning to the sweet smells of jasmine. I always knew my life's truth was somewhere not in that sweetness of a flower garden but rather on the hard concrete.

Life doesn't get back to "normal" after cancer. For me, it was a new chapter in the novel of my life. After the Chicago Marathon, I realized I couldn't fixate on looking in the rear-view mirror; it was time to focus on the life ahead of me.

It's Working For Me

I believe that if it were not for running, the world would be quite a different place for me. Running has become a large part of my life. My life chapters are full of the races I've completed and the friends I've met because of running. Days after running the Chicago Marathon, I felt complete. But my desire was incomplete. I quickly wanted to run another.

Once I had figured out how to make myself feel better, I had room to experiment with my perspective. After my life-saving surgery, I discovered that each day is a gift, and I was determined not to squander it. I had many friends and family who were frustrated about the price of college or complained about the weather. But I had a new perspective after surviving cancer, and things like this seemed to be trivial compared with the grand scheme of life. I did not sweat life's small stuff. I woke up every day and said, "God, thank you for another great day above ground."

Testicular cancer comes with an unforgiving stigma. Men may feel ashamed talking about something as private or as tied to their masculinity as the loss of a testicle. Some men don't want to go to the doctor. Their mindset is, "If we don't talk about it, then it's nothing to worry about." But all too often, they wait until something really dangerous is found.

Dr. K. told me that a high percentage of men with testicular cancer are much more likely to experience high levels of stress than with other cancers. I conclude that this was true for myself. He said one in ten guys will experience depression and may be afraid the cancer will come back in the other testicle. It was a roller coaster—one day I'd feel positive about life, and the next day I'd feel the exact opposite.

I also had to deal with my anger and the feeling that life was unfair. Why did I have to go through this? The thought of dating while going through testicular cancer was an experience. I feared what the cancer did or didn't do to my body, especially since I was so young. Would females worry about how the cancer might impact the relationship if they dated me?

After twelve months from the initial surgery, I no longer felt afraid of telling others about my diagnosis. I still felt emotional, but I was fortunate to have a fantastic support group. That gave me the confidence I needed to share my experience.

Today, I am left with occasional aches and pains, and once in a blue moon, I still struggle with not being in total control of my body. I'm no longer uncertain about the future, but I still find myself at times thinking about the past. I have a much better awareness of the importance of health and survival.

How Kaanapali Beach Changed Me

Having testicular cancer doesn't mean you can't travel. I learned how to make the most of life when my parents took me to Hawaii after my surgery. It was a vacation season just ripe for recharging my body. It was just what the doctor ordered after a difficult few months of facing uncertainty.

The best souvenir to myself was running on Kaanapali Beach, Maui's world-renowned beach. It was the most stunning three-mile beach I had ever encountered, and I ran every morning. I was relieved to be free of the daily mental stress. There was no doctor even close to this paradise. This much-needed trip was a reprise from all that crazy cancer testing.

My mind daydreamed as I took in the gardens, cool breezes, and stimulating scenes all around me. When I told a work colleague I was heading to Hawaii, he said to me, "You will be OK once you get there." Well, was he ever spot on with that! Before I left, I was tentative because all I had been involved with was tests and work. I hadn't taken any time for myself.

I was never a cynical person. But after my surgery, I saw every day as a struggle to get through. I used to not think that everything has a purpose. However, when life threw me a 125-mph curveball, reality sank in. My life now did have a purpose, and I realized that even the bad things in our lives can have an unseen benefit. By hindsight, all these years later, I understand clearly the good things that I came away with.

Surge

Once I returned from Hawaii, I focused on achieving my personal bests in 5k and 10k races. I began training with a professional runner who was sponsored by Brooks. I called him Surge because during every training run, he would surge ahead and try to bury me. It was his way of making me tougher on race day.

This new running partner was Italian. That made things good because while we stretched out, we would talk about all things Italian—making pasta, drinking wine, and our grandmothers being Italian. Surge truly helped me find myself with my running. He was the best training partner I could have had. We talked briefly about my cancer. He said that if I put it behind me and moved forward, both my running career and my life would come to fruition.

I remember laughingly telling him about all the dates I had with different girls. He said in a serious, sober voice, "One day you'll settle down." I lost track of him–life gets in the way. I think back now and credit Surge for showing me the way. What I truly regret about this time is that training with Surge didn't reflect on what else was happening in my life at that time. I needed to stop and look at the sunset and the life that I had yet to explore.

Surge was about nine years older than me. He had a family and a lovely wife. I looked at him as a good role model. Just like many cancer survivors, I was extremely nervous to return to racing in public. I acknowledged the butterflies in my stomach when I returned to competition after several months off.

We took off shirtless one Saturday morning for a six-mile training run. The temperature was a blazing-hot ninety-eight degrees. I'm sure you could have cooked a steak in a minute on the blacktop. After our run, Surge watched from a distance and then asked, "You okay?" He now understood me well enough to know not to smother me and instead observe me from a distance. Running from my past was hard, I thought that day. I felt exposed sharing many painful truths. I felt almost naked, thinking my nerves were raw endings for the world to see. Reliving many hospitals' recent memories was scary.

I can tell you personally what it feels like to be cut open like a can of tuna. How someone looks from the outside is not necessarily what they feel like on the inside. Especially when running shirtless throughout the streets in my hometown with a large protruding scar on my chest.

The Five-Year Reunion

It was my first five-year high school class reunion. I anticipated it being a great time. There was a DJ and dancing. When I walked up to the bar to get a drink, I turned to an old friend of mine to say hello. To protect the innocent, I'll call him Finch.

"Hey, I heard you got cancer from running," he said.

I said, "What in the world—who told you that? That's not how it happened at all."

From that moment on, my shoulders drooped, I felt disoriented, and I thought, *Wow. How could anybody actually believe that? As if you could catch cancer like the common cold.* I was thoroughly gutted that somebody would say that, much less a classmate who I'm sure heard from a friend, who heard it from their sister's cousin, who then stretched the truth more.

Who says something like that? Seriously, who? I've carried that pain with me for years. It formed far worse than scar tissue across my heart. I ended that summer with so much crossed off of my long-neglected to-do list and a lot of clarity about the future.

There were some hard things ahead, but I felt ready for them. This was my calling to a deep passion in life. I worked hard for the next five years. I searched for a life coach, who ended up being my very own doctor. Racing and having fun were essential. I came to know God much better. It took all of that to deprogram my mind from what the world said I deserved. It led to a place where I could have what I had only thought about in my wildest dreams.

At one with myself and God through running, the universe then delivered exactly what I needed. Mine is not an underdog story. Although my path was not clearly defined, I actually saw it as liberating.

After every track and cross-country meet in high school, I often thought my life would end up like a storybook. Cancer, though, would've been like being in the first Friday the 13th movie. I am writing this book as a way of becoming less afraid of what people say. Just to clarify, it all starts with facts and data.

I have this sense that the idea of drama and a serious illness was what led to this rumor that Finch heard. People weren't worried about whether what they heard was true; they just wanted to keep the story going.

Looking Back

Looking back, I wish I had owned my struggles and accepted them more. I didn't know what life had in store, or whether my scar would eventually be able to heal itself.

Because I had the abilities within me to get my life and career where I wanted it to be, I was able to envision my future, no matter my medical past. That feeling was the absolute best way to survive. I can laugh about all those anecdotes now. Running cures everything for me. Life is a marathon, something worth holding on to and celebrating at the twenty-mile mark.

Cancer didn't win. It tried and lost. Along the way, I had anxiety attacks and sleep issues. Some days, I would wake up feeling terrible, unrested, and unprepared to face the workday. I learned to see these as temporary flashes of unrest. They were all part of adapting to all the changes I'd gone through and learning to take one day at a time.

It's always acting from one's life values that balance is found. I'm now in a place I know well, having experienced it before. Encouragement, guidance, and moral support from others gave me the confidence to reach for my dreams and achieve them.

I was determined not to give up. I sacrificed the things I once thought I couldn't live without, and realized that was OK. That was part of growing beyond that safe place where fear is on the shelf. My hopes and dreams are covered with countless blankets. My stubbornness lies hidden within, cradled by my soft heart.

I think now and then about what would have happened if I were diagnosed with cancer while I was still in my teens. How would friends, teachers, and the community have treated me? Would I ever have run three marathons and two mini triathlons? Having cancer in the rear-view mirror often stirred an air of innocence in my soul. Those experiences certainly separated my world from those of my peers.

4

LIGHT A CANDLE

The day before learning that I would have surgery, my mother and father packed me in the car and off we went to our church. We each lit a candle and prayed to God. The lighting of a candle has more power than one believes. God is both personal and universal for many. In my experience of recovery, I learned to zoom in on the key characteristics I needed to focus on to better understand what was wrong with my body and brain, but faith in God was also key.

We lit candles, prayed novenas, Hail Marys, more Hail Marys, and more novenas. And after all was said and done, I was healthy as can be. If you looked at me, you would have no idea that I had just had a testicle removed. I learned to deal with painful things; the loss of a testicle was much like losing my pride.

I went through times of grief, yet I stayed humble. The lessons I learned helped me to experience humor in such a way that it helped me to express feelings in an attempt to get people to understand my situation. By laughing at myself, I showed those around me that I was confident enough to acknowledge my flaws.

Lighting those candles allowed me to feel life as a way of rediscovering it from the beginning. Going to a quiet place and being alone with God was very therapeutic. Every morning, going on a short run cleared my head. When I got to work, I would stare at the computer like I was in a trance.

I spent time wondering what life was going to be like now. Would tomorrow come? Who would I meet, and how would they see me? What had been taken from me provided a way for knowledge to extend through everything else in life. What I felt daily was important and relevant. Those experiences have stayed with me for a lifetime.

When self-apologies are genuine, they involve empathy and personal development. I focused on improving my performance through devotion. Lighting a candle was the best way to achieve my goals. I survived the several post-cancer years by changing long-held beliefs about what had happened and interactions that had taken place with people. With a conscious effort, I pushed past my pride to acknowledge my mistakes and make amends to those to whom I had not listened.

The school of hard knocks taught me that apologies are a sign of strength. Admitting wrongdoing was harder than I expected, though. *What will happen if, one day, this whole thing works out as I hope?* I wondered. I must say, lighting a candle every day was the reason my faith remained strong. *Would life give me empty promises?* I hoped to get the most out of my job, find a soulmate, get married, and start a family. It was best not to be stuck in a worrisome state of mind. I learned to accept peace and be in control.

Sometimes at night, when I closed my eyes, I struggled to piece together where I was in my mind. Some of the pieces didn't fit; it was just a bunch of faded memories. My lighting of candles created a lasting memory of an absence I had been experiencing. My personal statement is to not worry about things I cannot change. Today I work for myself. A wee candlelight can't hurt.

The Scar

"Don't be shy now," the nurse said. "Dr. K. did a very nice job with this."

I turned to my doctor and said: "As a concerned person, and as your patient, I ask you, without meaning to offend you, how did that long, snakelike scar on my stomach come to be?"

It was a fair question. Dr. K. was getting ready to assess things. Finally, the bandages were lifted, and I raised my clammy palm to wipe away my tears. Dr. K. paused, lost in some sensitive reflection. He had a look about him that was very somber.

The scar was very pink, a quarter-inch thick, thirteen inches long, and held together with eighteen staples. It went from my breastbone to my nether region. Dr. K. spoke with dignity about his work and the meticulous way he had carved around my belly button.

With this hideous scar, I felt the weight of the world bearing down on me. This huge scar affected me dearly, and it was all I could do to hold on tighter and tighter mentally and emotionally.

At times, my thoughts were taking over every waking minute, and they were all tied to my story and survival. My college classes, lectures, and social influences all helped me to grow up. I will never forget this time in my life.

I was faced with understanding and acceptance of what I had now become. But once I got the basic idea, I discovered that God's tastes are completely different from mine. Part of my problem was that my mind hadn't healed very well at that point. Anyone who has ever seen me without a shirt on could easily see the scar, and I was very self-conscious about it. However, since the surgery, several hundred folks have seen it at beaches, on vacations, and in gyms.

I have come to believe that I am a cancer warrior. I wear this battle scar with pride. Through my younger relationships, I suffered many scars, not visible, but more psychological. My physical scar is, quite simply, a reminder that I am still alive and living life to the fullest. I'm reminded daily that surgery left a visible scar. But it didn't make me a quitter. I will forever be known by a select few as the guy who has a scar the size of a pizza cutter.

But what about scarring? Was there some point when heading to the gym and showering that the scar would subside enough to not be overly apparent? I needed my friends' opinions and their wisdom. No one is immune from insecurity. I needed their approval. I needed someone to tell me it would all be simply fine in the end.

Sand It Down, Buddy

I now ponder those utterly quiet days and what I call fearful days. I was always thinking about the future and wondering whether another tumor was growing inside my body. After my surgery, I expected the world to be my saving grace. I thought that the reason this happened was to make me visualize my own existence. In my mind, God was saying that I needed to be an example of achievement and goals.

Reflecting back today, I'm not sure I was in the right frame of mind to expect anything. At twenty-one, I was high on life. I was naive in my thinking back then. I focused with every fiber of my being on nothing but the joy of being alive and seeing family and friends every day. I may have wandered, but I was never lost.

You know, when you're twenty, you don't usually think about being six feet under. Running with the autumn wind at my back, I took for granted the sky, trees, green grass, and the mere act of being outside. Some of my memories of that time are as cloudy as a cataract. I tended to see life through a filtered lens of music, alcohol, and parties. But that changed as I grappled with young adulthood, the scars of my childhood experiences, and the challenges of growing up in the 1980s.

Yes, my days were a little dark, but fortunately, based particularly on my surgery, I was able to bounce back in college. I developed less patience for nonsense, less tolerance for ineptness. I saw that so many people were wasting their lives. I was fueled by not listening to complaints and people saying useless things.

So, how did I go from my own ponderings and staring blankly at friends and strangers to pumping out miles on my hometown streets? I just went out and said to myself, "Go! Now! Run!" It was an attempt to unleash the rage and anger I felt.

It might not sound super earth-shattering or particularly insightful, but to me, it was a new perception. As I determined who I was, I was able to let go of all the expectations I'd been holding on to for so long, and the belief I needed to be something I wasn't. I discovered that I was my own saving grace.

About two years after the dreaded surgery, one Saturday night, Joe and I decided to go out and cruise our local Main Street. Our typical route was about a mile and a half down a two-lane avenue. Other guys were honking and yelling at girls. Many gals were spending time together at McDonald's and Steak 'n Shake.

Some kids would park in local businesses' parking lots and sit in their cars and people-watch. I found the city inspiring. That night, we did a little partying and then stopped in at the local pizza joint. There were some local college sorority girls at the next booth to us. Joe leaned over and struck up a conversation with them.

They asked where we went to school. Joe said he was trying out for the Chicago Bears. They giggled, thinking he was serious. The look on his face was so convincing, like having a heart attack. Then they asked about me. Joe said, "Oh, him, he's an adult dancer downtown at Big Alice's." Joe could make it all sound so simple. Thinking of myself with a long scar dancing for women was beyond my wildest dreams. It was funny... but not really funny.

We had some good laughs with those sorority girls. Then we paid for our tab and walked out to my car. While driving home, Joe turned to me in a very earnest voice and said, "You know, you can have your scar sanded down, Bri. It's minor plastic surgery that you'll hardly notice once it's done. This may be the perfect gig for you!"

But, for me, it was an extraordinarily complex discussion that had many layers. I felt the public didn't know much about my struggles, and it was better to keep it that way. If I did have my scar sanded down, I would still be the same person who had been through so much pain. That scar made my life a challenge.

Joe still laughs about that night. "They believed our story, Bri," he'd say. That night and those sorority girls are but a fading memory. There are times when I pause and wish I had sanded the scar down. Then again, this thirteen-inch scar is a reminder of my past and who I am today.

Thinking and Party Time

After my cancer, there were about ten more years of tests and follow-ups. I changed my major five times; it was like a revolving door. As I encountered life's challenges, the tried-and-true antidotes didn't always ease my feelings of despair. I stayed balanced with exercise as my meditation.

There was a favorite night spot, Sully's, where my friends and I would go to eat and drink and enjoy the merriment. It was open until 4:00 a.m., so there was no need to get there before 10:00 p.m. Sully's was a place of wild old times, dancing on tables, and unabashed life. I listened to people talk, I remembered things, and I felt things. Sully's was the spot to see and be seen. It was a late-night Irish pub in downtown Peoria, Illinois. The music started around 10:00 p.m., and it was the best eighties dance music you can imagine. Everyone knew the resident DJ, Fix. After a long week of college lectures and tests, it was high time to treat ourselves to some bevvies. Back then, every moment required attention. Music was a powerful and mysterious way we communicated with one another, the way we tried to describe our feelings.

After four-plus hours of dancing with many local college girls, I sat at the bar one Sunday morning with my friend. At 3:45 a.m., the owner, Mike (aka Sully Sullivan), leaned over from behind the bar and tapped my friend's shoulder, then mine. "Hey, guys, last call."

My friend raised his head like a tortoise, looked at me, and said, "One more for the road!"

We had a designated driver that night, our college friend B.B. liked to drink diet soda and people watch all night while we danced. As we walked to the car, I remember the wind as it rumbled in the sky that Sunday morning. I could see a distant flash of lightning as a summer storm rolled in.

On that particular night, we laughed wildly in the car together as we made awkward small talk about certain girls. That pre-dawn drive gave me permission to be free and unencumbered after a long night of drinking and dancing. Every weekend was the same. We were taken on a journey that felt like an engaging, provocative story. We were always ready to lose ourselves away from studying and working minimum

Light a Candle   65

wage jobs. Those nights were mindless offerings of an invaluable experience for us young twenty-somethings.

I remember those days as if it were yesterday. That eternal last call and a bottle of cold Budweiser. The incredibly fun times of the 1980s brought endless stories that will never be replicated again. What happened at Sully's stayed at Sully's.

The Unwanted Call

It was a warm, sultry August evening—the kind when you sweat after taking just two steps outside. I was out with friends. My father answered the call; it was Dr. K. He told my dad that he was leaving the practice and moving out of state with his family. I was devastated when I heard this news. I thought, *Now where is my life headed?* Dr. K saved my life, and he gave me a lot to think about. *Who would I go to now?* It was just a little over two years into my relationship with Dr. K.

My mother called her cousin Gloria, who worked in nuclear medicine at Pekin Memorial Hospital, where I had my surgery. Gloria said there was a great young new urologist here in town. She promised to call him and recommend that my records be sent to him and to accept me as a new patient.

From the first day I started seeing Dr. Joseph Banno, I knew that this was going to be a great patient/doctor relationship. I remember vividly the first time seeing him in his office. I was peering out the window in the waiting room when he drove up in an Alfa Romeo. He parked it while blaring the Rolling Stones. He proceeded to walk in with a pizza box in hand. I thought, *How cool—a pizza-eating urologist!*

A Little Advice

I wish I could give this little advice to all men. If you suspect something is wrong, don't wait—go to the doctor! Don't feel that you are weak. Seek help. If you wait before having something questionable checked out, it will only progress.

The first encounter with my new urologist, Dr. Joseph Banno, was truly a relief, as well as much-needed in my life. Dr. K had saved my life; he had run all those tests. He led the charge, and now Dr. Banno was going to finish this race with me.

I felt a little heartbroken thinking the relationship that Dr. K and I had was over, and he was no longer part of my medical team. Dr. Banno truly took me under his wing as a young, serious, and scared patient in need of his advice.

The fact that I'm part Italian and Dr. Banno is also Italian made it all the better for this doctor/patient relationship. He truly is a great doctor. He saw me from the very beginning for who I truly was, a scared young male testicular survivor.

I am very thankful that Dr. K did the proper thing by removing my testicle and then ran all the tests to save my life, and then handed the baton to Dr. Joseph Banno.

My Path Forward

Sometimes healing starts with guilt and consequences. After finishing the Chicago Marathon, I was on the verge of the extreme, but it very well may have been my plan to success. And still, every autumn on the second Saturday in October, I stop and pause to think about being able to run in the Chicago Marathon. I am very thankful to have completed the race. "If I didn't do it then, I may not be where I am now," I tell myself.

Running through the park in my hometown, I stopped at a drinking fountain and cried a little behind my sunglasses. I wasn't sad because I wanted to go back; I just couldn't believe that all of those days added up to... this?

Those precious years and miles I ran are now gone. Poof! In the blink of an eye. I remember thinking, *Well, what now? Exactly what do I have now? My own personal conscience and memories?*

I trusted my fears and not the truth of my body, with whom I had forged a lifetime of trust. Would running take away my fears of loss? I was searching for an emotionally satisfying connection. What I discovered was that what I thought was a loss was actually my gain. By accepting the scar, the experience provided me with a new road. I was alive! I was healthy and had so much to look forward to.

I became aware that solitude was the way of acceptance. Life was not greener on the other side. I was missing a part of who I was. My identity was running. I was the "rock 'n' roll runner." I became aware of this when I was twenty-one years old, and a sense of loyalty and family came over me. Sometimes people commented on how beautiful solitude was. To me, however, solitude always seemed to reply with a question. I tried to overcomplicate my own process by trying to take on too much. Always running more, training harder, getting overwhelmed with the idea of winning.

How could I continue the comfort of a daily routine? Sleep, run, eat, study. I learned that life's simple but important pleasures can be found by looking through the eyes of others. Being on autopilot wasn't necessarily a bad thing. My eyes were wide open in those days. I felt alive and told myself I deserved to live. And I would like to live BIG!

5

THE WAY CANCER SHAPED ME

My personal experience brought vividly to life the all-pervading turbulence of testicular cancer. Turns out that there was really only one question for me: *How to go about living?* During this time, my mind had the capacity to understand the force of cancer and the limits of humans to affect outcomes, but I was not prepared for what it would do to my mental state of health.

At times, just the culmination of pure exhaustion left me crumpled in bed. How could I continue with my daily routine? I was twenty-years-old, so I decided to concentrate on sleep, running, eating, and studying. This taught me that life's simple pleasures can be routine; going into autopilot wasn't a bad thing.

After running ten extra miles each week and a few sleepless nights along the way, I decided I needed a goal: to run a marathon. Feeling better and cancer-free was what I wanted. My strategy was to start by learning the fundamentals of my body and nurturing it. I did worry that every little ache and pain meant the cancer was back. Those days, when I was in and out of my cancer testing, I was always pushing my limits and trying to get back to where I once was as an athlete.

Several months of stretching my running distances and being given "clear" signals from my doctors gave me confidence in understanding what my body was telling me. I got around to confronting my running habits. I remembered Coach Mac from my high school days always saying, "Sluga, keep your arms down! Forge ahead!"

My social circle remained a constant source of inspiration and encouragement. I kept my business of knowing where I was going to myself. I tossed away all the grudges and all the negativity that had overwhelmed my life. I came to realize not everyone needed to know about my cancer survivorship. I was like a tree. I nourished myself every day and grew. Not everyone saw how much I grew, but I did, and my friends and family helped me become positive.

After all these years, that familiar feeling I once had during my freshman year of college has come back. That feeling of power and health. Health, not only in my body but in my mind. My faith as a Christian helped me know I was never alone. Through the years, I have seen the sun go down at the end of the day. Like the sun, I may be down, but I will rise tomorrow. God's grace helped me understand that I was not defeated.

I learned that life goes on, and not as I had planned on by making my own decisions. I now know that taking risks is part of the plan. I did fail at times. I changed my college major five times over ten years and partied more than I care to admit. It was all about trying to find meaning in life. I ended up discovering that my gut instinct (and my God) doesn't lie. It led me to believe in myself and my abilities. I could set lofty goals and achieve them. I could trust myself!

In contemplating who I am today, I've realized that cancer did not define me, but it did shape me. I've had a grand lifetime of being with great, supportive friends, family, colleagues, and the love of my life. That's not such a terrible position to be in. I'm learning more every day and still growing like a palm tree.

Corporate America

I felt that if I stayed in my little one-horse town, success would never happen for me. My bout with testicular cancer had put me one event short of disaster. My lymph nodes were in check, but I was missing a piece of me. That was a lot less glamorous than most people would have you think.

I grabbed cancer by the ball(s) and choked that beast. I spent time rocking in my chair watching my scheduled shows. Trying to be a normal guy again. One final attempt to put myself in a position where I could be closer to my goal of being a professional.

My ambition of becoming a coach didn't pan out. The artery of life suggested a bypass of faith, deep in my belly was the place of transformation. Like an autonomous car humming but always within grasp, I continued to hope and pray that my dream of a bright future was within reach. I knew that my new life going forward was much more than a goal.

My moral compass is my path to believe in a dream, with time to look over the cards I've been dealt. I could play to win with those cards. There were no jokers. I was charting a new course. I was the one now making all the important decisions.

When I finally graduated with a Bachelor of Science (BS) in Communications from a small, private university, I wondered, *Did I have the passion for a corporate position? Would the money and climbing the corporate ladder fulfill me?*

A chance at a job with a future was my plan to join life's true path. Even though my coaching dream did not come through, I will forever wear a smile and challenge life's failures.

I knew nobody was going to hire me because of my quick wit and vast amount of useless knowledge. My good friend Joe always told me, "Bri, get to it–it's now or never." I always listened to my father, but I never really heard him. I was scared at the thought of a corporate job; I was fearful I didn't have it in me. But as Coach Mac once told me, "Don't compare yourself to others; focus on the route, not the outcome."

I focused on my day-to-day and healing my mind. I worked on releasing the negative notions and moving forward. I discovered through trial and error that running wasn't my only outlet. A corporate position could work for me. I decided to go for it.

Conversations

In conversations with my former self, I tell of a life without standing still, a life that is yet evolving. I speak of happy-go-lucky moments when time passes and dreams gain strength and confidence. Before my cancer, I had a day-to-day routine. It was nothing out of the ordinary and remarkably simple. After my cancer diagnosis, I realized how precious life is. I was an avid outdoors person.

I used those days to run and bike as a way to relieve mental stress. The road and sky in the morning were my friends. They were always there. Sometimes the sun was out; sometimes there were clouds.

I used this time in my life for self-discovery. My "me time," my solitary morning meditation runs, became a stepping stone for moving forward. My friends, work colleagues, and family were all essential to my new mental health. I was easing into what my new life as a survivor would be.

Thinking back, I realize how lucky I was that I did not have a breakdown after everything I had been through. The local community was my backbone. I told myself that my past doesn't define me; it makes me a better person, a stronger one. I have a future, and that is all I can ask for.

Confusion on how to define my maleness was the best way to explain my feelings at that time in my life. That brings me to an essential matter.

Certain things become more indicative of being a man than just a testicle. I had always been a bit of a restless soul, always thinking life was rushing by. Now I realize that I can't outrun time, but I can work on my future self.

Cancer changed the entire trajectory of my life. Today, I'm content to go deeper to get to the truth. I've learned it's not about pushing boundaries with myself but rather about trying something new. Now, with my new passion for writing, I have the chutzpah to go for it anyway.

Fear

I learned after my surgery how to fight despite fear. Fear causes one to lose. I know now about losing. Fear holds the best of us back. Don't fear your passions by saying something that halts your progress. Focus on your strengths, not your weaknesses. Make fear into a positive encounter. Identify the right steps you can take.

I would never have completed three marathons, three mini-triathlons, earned my undergraduate degree, secured a good corporate job, married the love of my life, and pursued my MFA in creative writing during the COVID-19 lockdown if I had let fear get the best of me. From after my surgery to this very moment in my life, the only fight I fight is not being my best.

Fear is very real. It's that thing whispering in your ear that something isn't right. Fears can come up at any time in your life. They never completely go away. Yet, once you realize you can control them, it's a lot easier. Therein lies the clue. Things are going to be demanding, and then I am taken by surprise when they are not.

For instance, stress is a particular personal feeling. Remembering term papers and doctors' visits caused me stress. I no longer fear what is happening daily in my life. I am not afraid of death or dying. But I do look both ways before crossing the street. Fear is a common emotion and serves a purpose. I also do not fear cancer anymore.

I once felt fear about completing anything, feeling almost disconnected from everyone and everything. I remember once, before a high school conference race, Coach Mac said, "Don't fear what you can't see." How right he was! Why did I fear losing? It was the same thing I feared after my cancer. Would I lose my life—or worse, let fear win? The struggle to reach the goal of life was powerful enough to make me believe in myself.

Oh, how I wish I could go back to my past and not have been so full of fear. I wish I could go back in time. As I lay in bed several years after my surgery, I thought about the fear question. If I wanted to die, all I could have done was wait. But that wasn't in my DNA. Too many races to run, concerts to go to, and new friends to make. Well, what I believed was that I was meant to live.

My father told me that to be afraid is normal, but to let fear control you is harmful. The key to life is never focusing on what someone else is doing. Trust me, you'll be a lot happier.

Choosing to Live Life

I think choosing to live life depends on many factors, not just the living part, but specifically the living for better or worse. For me, though, survival was a huge plus. As a young and enthusiastic runner, I felt that I could share something with people to help them return to a better existence.

Dr. K. suggested I should choose to create a life that was deeper and more powerful than the life I had before cancer. Dr. K. knew that running was the focal point of my life, the basis of my life force. Running was my therapy, my emotional rescue.

Everyone says college is the time to make friends for a lifetime. I discovered the importance of community, not just drinking friends and all-night card games, but real-life experiences with true friends. This brought me a new way of looking at life after having faced testicular cancer. I remember being pretty befuddled by trying to just be myself. I was in the minority at college, and college friends can just be mean at times.

People told me that between age and testosterone levels, my physical and mental health could someday make me feel like a shell of myself. Life was passing me by like moving pictures on a screen. Those days shaped my imagination. Regaining my well-being was the one thing I knew I had to do. I began to open my mind and heart to the wonder of what it meant to be alive.

Dealing with my diagnosis and the aftermath of the physical side effects caused me much emotional distress. With some embarrassment, I listened to my conscience and faced the feeling of loss. I was a feisty teenager, and many things were beyond my comprehension. Some of which have taken almost two decades to reveal their deeper meaning to me.

Dr. K. wisely said, "You will need a roadmap that will lead you exactly to where you can start to live life." I wisely listened to him and did just that. I began to live a life that I truly deserved. It didn't happen overnight, but it happened—and it's still happening.

Opinions

People have their opinions, and so do I. After my surgery, everyone had an opinion—the doctors, my parents, my friends, even the girls I dated. I took too long to figure things out. What I do know is that my opinion is the one that matters most when it comes to my life.

I didn't turn out to be that corporate manager. I didn't coach younger runners. I never became a counselor, but I did learn to put pencil to paper, where I expressed all those thoughts, dreams, and opinions.

Everyone was giving me their opinion; however, I wasn't listening. Instead, I was navigating through distant memories. The threat of another cancer was deep within my brain and my heart. I was lost in my thoughts. My conclusion was to focus on myself while setting attainable goals. By believing in myself, I would get there.

When I started to realize that life wouldn't always be about running, I could be open to other possibilities. I knew one day my legs would slow; those medals and trophies would be few and far between. I needed to get serious about studying and finishing my degree.

At first, I didn't feel capable of setting goals. I told myself I wasn't gifted enough to do it. Once again, a little inner peace was needed. Nothing was going to stop me from being me. Running away was easy; doing something and going forward with it was much harder. I dug deep and found that if I decided to work for something, I could do it. If I could complete a goal, I could succeed. At times, I was confused by people's opinions. I thought that somehow, whatever other people thought might come true and override what I thought.

I learned that I didn't need to convince other people that I was worthy of their time and admiration. I had my own personal reasons for putting myself and my opinions on an empty pedestal, too high to reach. If you were to ask me if I am content with my place in the world, and I said yes, that would be a big, fat lie!

All the while, I told myself I had a plan, and I was going forward with it. Truth be told, I ended up losing my creative drive and passion for competitive running. I was less and less content with things that used to make me happy. Which, I now realize, is just a long way to say: Opinions are subjective.

Patience, My Son

I've learned a great deal about patience in direct relation to life. One big realization is that being a cancer survivor is forever. This is not something that is easy to learn or come to terms with. You can't buy patience. It's that secret knowledge that comes with age and experience.

After racing marathons, I learned the importance of patience. I became submerged in the profound stillness of my past, present, and future. To put it simply, the race itself requires patience.

Patience is not unusual. It's as old as time itself. What I have learned about patience is to train my memory of events to recall when I was under pressure, and then listen to my thoughts and feelings. I remember my parents telling me, "If you have patience, you can have it all." Patience is a gift, and not everyone has it.

Patience is an instrument that needs to be fine-tuned. It's a trained emotion. Never think it's just another urge; instead, nurture it and take care of it. Give it the place it deserves in your life. Your mind needs uplifting and interactive experiences to deal with any persistent thoughts.

Sometimes, I found myself surrounded by people who had stress in their lives, and this drained my energy. I needed patience to walk away from those people. I would courageously ask myself, "Is this how I want to live? I deserve to live life to the fullest!"

Training for and running a marathon really taught me patience. A marathon is like life, a long, steady course with lots of obstacles along the way. I wasn't born with patience, but I've attained it through trust and determination. Aside from taste and smell, patience should be the most essential ingredient in the recipe of life.

6

HAPPY DAYS

Running: A Gift Against Weakness

Running has taught me how to overcome weakness by training and pushing my body; life is like that too. The lessons I've learned through running apply to so many other areas of life. Running taught me that I didn't know I could master weakness until I tried.

I've always had a love of music. I discovered that by exploring a song's meaning, its power pulled on my emotions. So many songs I knew from the past would pop into my head during my runs, and often the lyrics would affirm to me what strength and perseverance meant. As I listened in my head, I would no longer feel weak.

After my cancer, I experienced weakness caused by my mental state of recovering from my surgery. With no playbook on how to deal with something like this, it's important to know it looks different for everyone. Weakness is not always easy to recognize. I always put on a brave face, so people tended to see my smile and think everything was

OK. Yet inside, I was yearning for someone I trusted to see the inner pain I kept hidden.

I have gathered my focus through the years of recovery and healing. I've gone through life, living it rather than serving as a weak link. This experience opened a new path for me, allowing me to forge my own way. Let's be honest, talking about testicular cancer isn't a glamorous conversation. But how one deals with it can be huge.

Some of you reading this may be wondering whether you would even recognize the symptoms. My mom knew how hard it was on me as a young man after my surgery. In the spring, she would say it's a beautiful day for a run. She encouraged me to be fearless, and I dove head-first into the fray.

Whatever weighed on me and frightened or annoyed others would feel like a challenge. Being stable and consistent was what helped. I often felt like a radio with a frequency of feelings and energy that altered thoughts of my own reality. I became overcome at times. My flustered brain gave way in any given high-pressure situation.

My emotions associated with running were a critical component of my recovery strategy. I flourished with a presence of support; that was my therapy. Through some long, grueling years, I fought through my weakness. I created a space where I could take my feelings and pack them away. I was my own competition with everything: school, running, and relationships.

I grew from breaking the isolation that often came from self-doubt. I tended to trust everyone, and I chose not to see this as a weakness. I always tried to make sense of what had happened and how I could rid myself of trauma in the future. I prayed often that I would discover ways to leave the past in the past and push forward to a bright future. I learned not to take for granted simple pleasures, such as ice cream on a summer day, popcorn at the movies, or a date with a high school sweetheart. All of these everyday experiences made me realize how much I cherish life. Now, in my cancer-free years, I have many memories that I will never forget. I have never returned to the past, though–I live in the present.

I don't care about the word *weakness* anymore; it has a hidden quality of seeming judgmental. I discovered the path to overcoming a weakness was finding the deepest possible meaning in my life. I found myself in a place where there was no help, no one to talk to on a professional level, without paying a lot of money. Mental health was something people whispered about in private. Today, there are thousands of licensed therapists who are skilled in terms of unique needs.

Through all that, running was my saving grace. It was the therapy I could afford. It was where I could put my worries behind me. Running saved me and helped me cope with whatever I was stressing about at the time. I have my parents and good friends to thank for that gift.

A Good Cry

For many years, I suppressed my urge to cry. I always had preconceived notions about how crying made men seem weak. A runner who was a survivor shouldn't give away his own feelings. I do remember breaking down in the hospital days after my surgery. In such tense situations, crying is not a great vibe to have. But I have discovered that good things can come from crying.

When I was young, I remember hearing a middle school track coach saying that boys don't cry. Thinking I wasn't born yesterday, I knew that babies cry, and many people also cry when someone dies. When I was a sophomore in high school, my Italian grandmother died in her sleep from a stroke. I remember crying in that early morning, full of shock and dismay. Each time I remember her, I fight to hold back my tears.

I experienced a profound mind-body connection that evoked a range of emotions. I told myself not to worry about what I cannot control, and this relaxed my mind. I had a few things I needed to work out on my own. Crying was my vessel for expressing myself. I felt it as a cleansing, emotional experience. When I cry, it's the way my body purifies itself. If you feel anxious, stressed, or unclear about your personal health, I recommend letting the tears fall like a waterfall. Then you will find peace with your emotions.

Life doesn't come with a parachute. Crying on my training runs became my meditation. It was a cheap therapy session that helped me deal with anxiety and stress levels.

Sometimes, lost in the moment on a daily run, I would suddenly realize I had tears running down my face. When I ran, my guard was lower, I had a bit of brain fog, and memories of happy moments running by places brought me back to my childhood. Cancer was no longer my nemesis; now it was a time of reflection. When I was feeling like crap or the weather was horrible, running also gave me a huge emotional lift.

Running is like a much-needed relief you don't get when there are people around. It's a self-cleansing thing. Everything that's bottled up begins to come out. You feel aware of everything you had been ignoring. Even now, every time I have a good thought, a happy thought, or even a sad thought, I have a good cry.

My Mornings Are Broken

Morning often signifies rebirth and growth. I am usually happiest at that time. The disappointment of yesterday is behind us, and we are starting a new journey on a different day. I often remember Cat Stevens' song "Morning Has Broken." That old English Christian hymn was and still is part of my being. It's ageless, uplifting, and grounds me.

Can I trust my memories of when I was grieving the loss of my testicle? What was lost in that grief led me to a better understanding of the unpleasant consequences of my story. The period that followed was foggy, and mornings were always the best for me to think through the meaning of things for myself.

I could barely remember some of the moments that scarred me during my cancer treatment years. I had tucked them so far back in my mind that it took days for them to come out. What sounded like a triumphant moment, at the time, made me feel lost and depressed. I had no idea what my next move would be.

Typically, after a morning run, I think about the rest of the day. I would ponder whether something profound might happen during the upcoming hours of the day. I came to realize that money and popularity didn't matter. It was what was in my soul that made me who I am. During those moments of silence, I no longer thought about survival but rather living. As my mother told me when I was in grade school, "If you have good health, you have everything." I focused on taking good care of myself so I could live fully and well.

I now engage with real people who inspire me to embrace the night that is to come. Past dreams regenerate me as I imagine being surrounded by a new day. I've overcome the most common challenges that I faced when I encountered adversity. I learned how to be grateful for a new start. Even things that seemed too big before, I can now tackle. I have become a more positive person because of what I went through.

The loss of a vital part of me wasn't as bad as I had feared. Don't get me wrong, it was still horrible back then. But it wasn't the monster I had created in my head. Eventually, I was able to find peace. I had to look forward in order to see the hand I'd been dealt. I went through hard things and had nightmares, but I'm now a much humbler person. Cancer changed me. It made me realize that if I don't go out and do something, tomorrow may never come. The problem is as sharp as a cutting knife. I like to think I was not broken, but a ready-made patient man.

I Dreamed in Color

I didn't always dream in color. After testicular cancer, my life was fragile, complex, and often overwhelming. What I needed was someone who could give me a butt-kicking without actually doing it.

You might not believe this, but there is no such thing as a guilty pleasure. I discovered one must be ready to uncover the things that have been kept secret for so long, like the confidence to seize the day. It spawned an endorphin feeling inside me.

Silence helped me to deal with my fears and influence others. My spiritual strength helped me to maintain a sense of hope. I found courage in the face of a disease that was out to destroy everything.

I dreamed of a vision that hadn't yet occurred. Colors of light, I was in the dark, waiting for grief that would not arrive. Then I had an epiphany: I didn't need to live a life of emptiness; I could build a life full of peace and color. This brought me back to a life I always wanted. To seal the deal of my intention, I started up the hill and have never looked back.

Interestingly enough, as a starting point, my dreams in color showed me an understanding of what my life symbolized. Dreaming in color helped me make sense of being at peace with my surroundings and what I had been through. It helped brighten my days from the darkness I'd been experiencing.

The song "True Colors" was a number-one hit in 1986. The imagery of that song painted a picture in my mind. It encouraged me not to give up. I overcame my fear of not winning in life to become courageous and find happiness again. I discovered that life was always shifting. Focusing on my dreams brought me out of nothingness and into a new reality.

Running with No Regrets

I don't regret the things I did, but I regret a few things I didn't do. I regret not studying harder in high school. I also would have loved going out for the debate team. I always enjoyed communication and writing, but back then I didn't pursue this—I was what they called a jock.

I loved going to concerts and listening to my rock music on my headphones while running in high school. I didn't take it seriously at the time, but the 1980s were a great time to grow up.

I went on midnight runs alone. I ran in nighttime storms and lived to talk about it. At times, my emotions about having one testicle were unbearable, especially living in a community where everyone knew my name. It was as if I were running up a mountain. Thinking about my future was a challenge: Would I have children, start a family, or just be single and live out my days?

Dr. K. had removed a testicle, and although I was incredibly happy to be alive, I wondered about what-ifs. He offered to put a prosthetic testicle; this would be a cosmetic procedure for looks. I said most definitely not! There would be no surgery to put a fake testicle in my body.

Decades passed, and my ability to have children was slipping away. At that time, I didn't know if I wanted children, but I wished Dr. K, my parents, my friends, and my priest had opened my eyes to the option.

I just assumed that my sperm was as healthy as the sperm of any other young man. Yet research has proven this to be false.

From the age of forty, men produce less sperm, due to age and genetics. I came to the realization that what was going to happen would happen. I regret not banking my sperm. All I ever wanted in life was to have a sibling. And I thought about what it would be like if I were to have a child. I'm sure the price of banking one's sperm is not cheap. But at the time, I wouldn't have cared. I would've gone ahead with it.

As a testicular cancer survivor, I was monitored more. I'm grateful for all the follow-up care to check for any recurrence. I thank God daily for my good health. But for decades, I hid my daily anger and anxiety from everyone. I was concerned about my self-image and life changes. One's inability to father children can contribute to anxiety or depression. Every month is a day of celebration for some, while for others, it may be a day of suffering. I've learned to celebrate being alive every single day.

Today, I am not only enjoying my life but also appreciating it. I look for the simplest treasures and have gratitude. I notice the positive things and feel the goodness life has to offer. What I may have lost by not having children, I have gained by being present every single day.

What I was seeking was always right there in front of me. After I met the love of my life and got married, I realized there was a purpose for me. Being childless wasn't the end of the world. It was the beginning. I still have no regrets. Life is good, and I am alive.

Actions and Decisions

My actions and decisions after cancer were life changing. What resonated with me was competing in 5 and 10ks; those races are what made me a better person. Competing in them gave me a purpose. They are what made me a better person. Running gave me a purpose, and winning trophies and medals increased my self-worth.

Running is a lonely sport. However, road racing is exhilarating competition at its finest.

Time has a way of catching us unaware. We wonder, *How did I get where I am now?* The secret is finding a way through the world's madness. Heartache happens to everyone, and it can be bigger than life at times. We all need humility and simple pleasures to get us through life's chaos.

As you begin to lessen the tension, the process can start to tell you something about yourself. I valued what I know that changed the way I see and live in the world. I had finished the race; I had completed the test before me. My race was one of endurance. I followed my doctors' orders and worked out a plan for exercise and diet. I figured out a way to get the prize of "all clear," and I refused to look backward. I came into my own, and it was astonishing.

My Plan to Write It Down

As anyone fighting testicular cancer—or any other form of cancer—will tell you, it is through the fear and the pain that one rises up. Personal outbursts go with the disease. After my surgery, I had an extraordinarily strong sense of courage deep inside my soul. With the decision to remain positive, my passion for running and competing helped me face and win some of the biggest battles of my life.

Running helped to overcome the illusion of complete solitude. That community helped me to think less about my inability to have children and the feeling of loss I associated with having only one testicle. I spent months prepping for perfection, yet I missed wisdom. My plan was to be positive and connect with myself and with others.

Then it hit me: Write it all down. This was based on my coming to terms with silence. How you communicate is a little like deciding what to wear. It can make you the most noticed person in the room. I decided I wouldn't be afraid to ask for what I wanted. I know that time is on my side. I cried out to survive the stuff mountains are made of.

Feelings of enormous gratitude allowed me to plan for my days, my time, and my happiness. Friends, family, faith, and doctors helped me through this journey. Writing about my experiences helped me remain focused and able to navigate the realities of the world.

Sharing my life through my daily writing is my personal plan for success. Staying with it is often more of a mental chore than a physical one. The key to a good plan is pushing yourself on your "down in the dumps" hard days while being stress-free on relaxed days.

There are some interesting parallels between memory and planning your future life. For example, I am beholden to my childhood Language Arts teacher who had the class repeat the mantra: "Never give up! Make good choices!" As this stuck in our minds, we began to realize that we were young at heart, but our future was still at hand.

I still remember someone telling me about a movie called *Brian's Song*. I researched it, and I was surprised and sad about how it ended. I discovered it was the tragic story of a young athlete dying of testicular cancer, more than a decade before my diagnosis. This was at a time when discussing testicular cancer was taboo.

No one had told me that this film would cause me to cry. My own story concludes with a dream in which I am in a book that nobody will ever be able to finish. I wave to the crowd and go away, always known as a victor. Yet moving through the years, I find myself in an uneasy state with my own experience of testicular cancer. Nothing anyone can do or say will make it better. I've struggled with how to balance optimism with self doubt. I address that struggle daily as a writer. I have choices and take my chances even if at times they are ill-advised.

All Said and Done

I am convinced the best time to bury something is after you're finished with it. I am long since finished with cancer. I am here and responsible for all I have said and done. I did squander opportunities at times. Though it is all the light and dark, the rain, the storms—I have found peace with myself. Everything that happened, all my conversations with doctors, friends, and relatives—I now know they were all for the better.

Those moments remain special and helped me find peace within myself. Everything I've gone through has given me the courage to tell my cancer story and share my journey.

Nothing matters more than being able to understand one's growth through the pain. Regardless of your situation, one's mental and emotional state is the most crucial factor in all life's problems. I developed a belief system to achieve my self-worth. I am in control of outside influences.

It's possible you'll get lost along the way. I've thought about what I would do if I had to do it all again. In a nutshell, I would have made more friends and worried less. I am spitballing here, but when I finally heard the whispers of my own truth, that's when I knew that the voices of others were chasing after me. Whispering to myself what I wanted, it took years to separate who I am from the pack.

It took many long nights to learn that we aren't all made from the same cloth. What was the worst thing that could happen if I listened to my own voice? Did I really want complete strangers to sum up my life? As friends and runners converged on me, the distractions didn't help. Self-pity was not in my DNA.

The light in that room was turned on, but it is now off. I'm no longer asleep—I'm wide-awake. I no longer want to mention loss, hate, or disdain for anything. I don't live in fear. My past experiences proved to be just examples of my past self and nothing more.

I was clear of self-doubt and pushing forward. I look back on my past as a complex college exam, one I passed with a perfect score. Now it's time to move on to the next course. From grade school to high school to college and into adult life, I was a star athlete and competitive runner. But that is all in the past. My life and situations are much different now. There were highs and lows, bumps and bruises. In addition to testicular cancer, I've had basal cell skin cancer and had to deal with three meniscus tears in my knees. So, no more competitive running. No more mini triathlons, 5ks, 10ks, or marathons. It's the end of the road for me on that journey. My new motto is "Who dreams wins." Now I take my racing bike out and explore the beautiful Florida coast.

Seeing the results I had aspired to are no longer distant. Cancer didn't win. I grabbed cancer by its horns. It was my nemesis, my Goliath, and I was David. I kicked it without thinking of the consequences to my body. When all was said and done, I was the victor in the battle.

I've learned amazing lessons from my life experiences and from coaches, friends, colleagues, and fellow runners along the way. What they taught me about never giving in or giving up has shaped me into the person I am today. I found my lost cheese, and now I can help others to find theirs. That thirteen-inch scar is but a battle wound. I've developed the right balance between maintaining past experiences and bringing in fresh ones.

When all is said and done, it is not the past that defines me; it is my future. I know that now, and without realizing why, I try to avoid all the things that tempt me. Along the way, we must all collect a lifetime of understanding. Most people don't spend a lot of time thinking about time. But time is not a luxury; it's actually a necessity.

I have now found that my search for peace and contentment was not about anything from my past. My truth was hidden in my silent voice. Now is the best time to leave all I have been through in the past and embrace the unknown future. I remember that shriek, but I will never let it ruin my future self.

7

DATING AFTER CANCER AND MEETING MY PERFECT MATCH

Body image has a significant impact on how a person feels about being intimate and interacting with partners. In my case, at times I felt embarrassed or ashamed. I worried that my partner would look at me differently.

It was touchy to discuss this aspect of my body with a potential partner. I wondered if this would cause concern in a potential romantic relationship. The decision about exactly when to tell that special someone that I only have one testicle was a difficult one. Would they think I was less of a man? They would think I might not be able to produce children. Let's face it, many women in their twenties and thirties are thinking about marriage and a family sometime in the future.

With all that I had been through and just getting settled into a normal lifestyle, marriage was not at the forefront of my mind. I thought about it at times, but not continually. I discovered it was normal to feel a lack of confidence, whether or not someone had one testicle or two. Sex can make us feel vulnerable and anxious that something might go wrong in the bedroom.

Remember George Costanza on Seinfeld and how self-conscious he was? The revelation that television could portray self-doubt seemed to stir up as much surprise as the realization that I was not alone. At the time, there was no one really that I was serious enough about to discuss my condition, apart from my urologist. I wasn't about to go up to a potential partner and say, "Hey, I only have one testicle—what do you think?"

No one can see my scars or that I'm missing a testicle. And I don't think having only one testicle is bad. The decision to share this with someone is a very private one. It's made me realize how deeply we all long to be truly seen for ourselves and accepted.

I learned to accept my body, and it humbled me. While some days are hard, I no longer hang my head in shame. Looking back, I do wish I'd had more of a support system so I could have talked about my feelings. So, if I can offer some advice, it is to simply ask for help and not be afraid to talk to your partners about what to expect.

Meeting My Match

After several decades of working the corporate life, I decided I was ready to settle down and get married. I had dated regularly since my testicular cancer discovery, so it wasn't like I hadn't tried. Countless females throughout the years were just not the right fit. Of course, finding the right person is not like a job interview. It's a lifetime commitment.

Friends would fix me up on dates. They would say, "She is nice; she likes sports like you. We think you will get along great." I learned the hard way that this can be code for "She is obsessed with her body and looks" or "She is a daddy's girl." With most of them, I had no connection, or they would tell me, "You're just too outgoing." I found myself wondering, *if I was ever going to settle down, did I need to change?*

Then one day, I overheard a work colleague in the coffee kiosk at work telling another colleague that they had met someone online.

I had recently investigated Yahoo Personals. I had several dates for coffee and conversation that just did not work out. I decided that I could keep trying with conventional dating methods, knowing it could take many years and end with zero success. Or I could go all out and try an out-of-the-box approach. I was always the guy to try something new, so I decided to give it one more whirl. I joined Match.com, which was a new site at the time.

Many of us might not be willing to try online dating, but I had faith that my true love was out there. And what does a Midwest boy do when he finds himself with unfinished business? I saw myself on a journey, intertwined with an adventure of fate. My heartbeat sped up just thinking of a bright future with someone who had a dream of seeing the world and chasing the stars.

My father told me when I was in high school that women are life's greatest mystery. Figuring them out requires curiosity, vision, and wisdom. Boy, was my father ever spot on!

It took me quite a bit to learn about life, experience, and emotion. I am proud to have seen my parents' marriage, and I wanted to experience something just as beautiful in my life.

A woman named Maureen and I had exchanged messages back and forth on Match.com for about a month. I finally told Maureen my first name and that I worked for Caterpillar Inc.. Little did I know she also worked for Caterpillar Inc..

Our first date lasted six hours and thirty-five minutes. First, we met for dinner at Keleher's on the Peoria downtown riverfront. Maureen got there first and called me to say she was in the parking lot. "Where are you?" she asked.

I said, "I'm on my way, just running a little late. Please wait for me in the parking lot." She did wait, although a bit reluctantly. When I arrived, I was met with an unbelievably cute brunette standing by her car, a ragtop Volvo. She was suntanned and had a bubbly smile.

Over dinner, we discussed our education and career aspirations. She had received her MBA at the same university where I got my undergraduate degree. We talked about our families and what we liked to do and not do. I told her I was an only child. During the course of our conversation, Maureen didn't get up and run out, which I took as a particularly good sign. We discovered that, besides being Catholic, we also shared a love for live music and enjoyed dancing.

From that evening on, I knew that this woman was quite different than the rest of them.

The Next Date

For our second date, I agreed to meet Maureen for lunch at Buffalo Wild Wings on a Sunday afternoon. We met some of her friends there. We ate and watched the St. Louis Cardinals versus the Chicago Cubs. Maureen was a Cardinals fan, just like me. In Illinois, the Cardinals and Cubs are a big rivalry, and I figured that this Redbird fan was one I wanted to pursue.

The next Friday night, we went out for Mexican food and a movie. Maureen shared with me on this date that she had checked me out on the Caterpillar Inc. directory. I had previously shared with her that I was the secretary on a Caterpillar Inc. volunteer board called Community Now, and she used that information to start her detective work. She knew my first name from our email communication through Match.com, and she looked up an old Community Now newsletter and found my full name listed as one of the board members. She then looked me up in our workplace directory. My photo was not included in this directory for some reason. Curious if she might know anyone in my workgroup, she then clicked on my supervisor's name, but she didn't recognize him. She proceeded to the next level of management, and bingo, it was a friend of hers with whom she had previously worked at Caterpillar Inc..

Next, Maureen called her friend, tactfully trying to ask about me. Her friend, my manager, finally asked, "Are you trying to steal Brian away from me?"

Maureen confessed, "No, I met him online and wanted to know if he lived with his mom in the basement and was a kitten killer."

My manager laughed and said, "Oh no, he has a heart of gold."

Just 128 days after our first date, I accompanied Maureen and her mother to Saint Louis, MO to celebrate Christmas with her family. On the drive down, Maureen's mother grilled me pretty thoroughly. She asked me if my parents were practicing Catholics, and she wanted to know where I attended church. She was wondering how serious a relationship this would be. She inquired about why I wasn't married and asked me what kind of work I did. I also shared with her that I had testicular cancer as a young twenty-year-old, but I was currently cancer-free and healthy.

As you can imagine, meeting Maureen's nieces and nephew for the first time was very intimidating. This was the first time that Maureen had ever brought a boyfriend to a family function, and they, too, had many questions for me. They took turns asking where I worked, if I was a sports fan, what I thought about the St. Louis Cardinals, if I liked dogs or cats better, and so on. It was as if I were at a job interview.

When they found out I was Catholic, a lifelong Cardinal fan, and genuinely liked their aunt, it eased their concern.

It was intense, but they only wanted what was best for their daughter, sister, and aunt. Most families want the best for their daughters. It is a tough world out there. They knew how ambitious Maureen was and wanted her to be with a guy who could keep up with her. I made sure they all knew how much I liked Maureen and would always be respectful of her, which in the end, was the most important thing to them.

I had been wanting to find a special person who would add fun and love to my life. Maureen was that person. Cancer is a topic that can be discussed without frightening people. Just stick to the facts. You do not have to share every detail; an acknowledgment that you suffered and are now feeling healthy is all that is necessary. In my case, I realized that Maureen's family just wanted to know that their loved one was in responsible hands and safe.

It takes a bit of faith and courage to date a cancer survivor. If you feel like you are being grilled about it, be mindful that the questions are out of love to really understand you and not just mere curiosity.

For a genuine, long-lasting connection to take place in your life, you need to be honest with yourself and your partner about your cancer from both a physical and mental state.

Happily Ever After

We had talked about marriage months before I popped the question, and we had even looked at rings together. Maureen and I are both traditional, and there would be no announcement of intended marriage until I proposed, but nothing had been set in stone.

After dating a total of 1,351 days from August 17, 2007, to July 9, 2011, I finally made the decision to propose to Maureen. I went back to our local jeweler and picked out the perfect ring. I had it mounted as she had wanted. There was a newly opened upscale restaurant in her hometown. I called a month in advance and told him what I was doing, and he booked a table for me. I had it all planned out. Everyone from the maître d, the waitstaff, and the manager on duty was in on it.

After work, I stopped at the jewelry store and picked up the ring. To my delight, it was in a nice, cushioned pouch with a red ball tied around it. Mo's father had suddenly passed years before we met, so I planned to go to see her mother and ask her permission for Maureen's hand. I arrived at her mother's condominium, not realizing she was hosting her bridge club. I rang the doorbell and asked if I had permission to marry her daughter. Immediately, tears began rolling down both our cheeks.

We were still standing in the foyer when she said, "Come on in, please." As I walked in, I gazed at seven women at two tables playing bridge. She introduced me and told everyone what I had come for. They all got up and were so excited to see the ring.

Later that night, I got on one knee and asked Maureen for her hand in marriage, and she said, "Yes!" I had to take a moment to catch my breath. Just like when I first saw her, it was as if time stopped. There seemed to be significant love between us, more than life itself.

We chose April to get married because it is a beautiful month, with trees and flowers beginning to bloom. Two priests performed the ceremony. As a Catholic, I had often thought of the verse when God said, "It is not good that the man is alone," as Adam slept in Eden. "I will make him a helper like himself." It is that exact verse that makes me believe and feel complete. We both draw strength from that verse and from each other, knowing we are one forever. We feel safe and secure with each other.

To our surprise, after three years of married life, Maureen got a chance of a lifetime—an international assignment that took us to Belfast, Northern Ireland. After three and a half years, we repatriated to Houston, Texas, and finally to a new corporate office in Irving, Texas. It has been one heck of a ride. Maureen has shown herself to be a true inspiration to me and to our family and friends.

I thought of online dating as the end of the line, but in our case, it was just the start of something big. I am grateful for the lessons learned and the support Maureen has given me.

Since my cancer diagnosis, the innocence of my life was like viewing my world through a grain of sand. It is the significance of the universe poured into one tiny grain. Like one little tumor, one little growth. I have learned so much on my journey, and I hope my story has enlightened you and opened your eyes as well as your mind.

AFTERWORD

I have come to see that each struggle in life is a crossroad, involving friendships and acquaintances of all backgrounds. Rather than think of this as goodbye, I invite all who have shared in my journey to look deep inside, find the truth, and live their best life.

Taking permission is a synonym for one's identity. When thinking of identity, think of living and connecting yourself with an experience. The world is a better place since I have learned to face my fears and disappointments and embrace hope. By believing and never giving up, I will continue to be even more resilient.

If you want to have a chosen life, you'll have to work extremely hard. I didn't believe that when I was a kid. Working hard in life is not something you can get from a vending machine. I learned that if I worked hard, I would find success. I realized that if I were going to make it, it would be due to my honest work and my clear determination.

I have learned through life to be a fighter—that failure is not acceptable. All those long winter runs in high school and after my cancer helped me see that education and studying are an exercise in overcoming stress through my mindset and determination.

I want to stand up for testicular cancer patients and survivors. To say I owe it all to my doctors, parents, and friends is not enough. If you ever find yourself lost, may you find comfort in the sure-footed life experiences of others. May they help you find your way, and may they be a light for making your way through the uninhabited imagination of your world.

I've run road races, marathons, biked, and competed in triathlons. Yet remembering everything I've gone through on my cancer journey was by far the most difficult challenge of all. I want to spend my future living a normal life, filled with writing, traveling, and spending time with my friends and family, not running away from or living in fear of this dreaded disease called testicular cancer. Maintaining close connections with others has been good for my mental and spiritual well-being. I hope this book will reconnect me with friends I haven't interacted with for some time.

The stories in this book remind me that I am a survivor, and that makes me smile every day.

With an optimistic outlook combined with confidence, life has given me a sense of power. I no longer take moments for granted. I'm grateful for the good things that are still in store for me. This is not because I haven't experienced professional challenges or hardships. I have never experienced anything but challenges.

What I have learned in my life since cancer is that things can change in an instant. That's why it has been so important for me to connect with people who inspired me to grow, being able to share my experiences with people who understand. In introspection, I took a deep dive inside myself to find out what I wanted and what I was.

Many people are unsure of what they want or lack clear life goals. For me, I chose not to be a prisoner of my past. Cancer wasn't going to detract from the good times. Those special moments were not going to snatch away my innocence. On this path, I found aspirations, dreams, and everything else I needed to achieve on this journey.

I went through many times of confusion, but that's over now. I've experienced things few my age ever will. These experiences have made me stronger. In my younger days, life was a wild ride, but I always managed to stay on track. I choked back tears, recalling the little voice at the end of the day that said, "Don't fret over the little things."

*Words bring imagination to life, they are like wings
that have no limits, a journey to a new world.*
— Brian T. Sluga

ACKNOWLEDGEMENTS

A special thank you to my best friend, Joe Gianessi. He has been with me throughout this journey and has been a God-send in my life.

Thank you to Steven Crocker from the Testicular Cancer Awareness Foundation for his support. Catch his interview with me on his podcast, "It Takes Balls".

Thanks to Terri Snow, MD, and Judson Snow, MD, for their support, encouragement, and advice in writing this book.

Thank you to Claudia Volkman, owner of Creative Editorial Solutions, for being a great editor and friend.

Thank you to Joseph J. Banno, MD, Midwest Urological, Peoria, Illinois for being the best urologist a young patient could have during those cancer years and still is today in my "mature" years.

ABOUT THE AUTHOR

Brian Sluga is an award-winning writer, blogger, cancer survivor, and customer experience consultant. He has written two books, and his poems have been published in a variety of books and magazines.

Brian was raised in Pekin, Illinois, and graduated from Bradley University with a Bachelor of Arts in Communications. He also earned a Master's degree from Lindenwood University in 2022, where he honed his writing skills. When not traveling, Brian resides in Naples, Florida, better known as "Paradise," with his wife, Maureen.